Un-American Education:

THE
over-schooling
AND
under-educating
OF
America

Daniel M. Hagadorn

Un-American Education: The over-schooling and under-educating of America

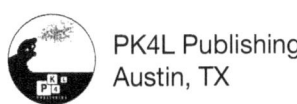 PK4L Publishing
Austin, TX

Copyright © 2014 by Daniel Hagadorn

All rights reserved, including the right to reproduce this book or portion thereof in any form whatsoever. For information, address:

Daniel Hagadorn
www.PK4L.com
www.welcomePK4L.com

Every attempt has been made to source all quotes correctly.

For additional copies or bulk purchases visit:
www.amazon.com/author/danielhagadorn

ISBN: 0-615-97811-8
ISBN-13: 978-0-615-97811-6

10 9 8 7 6 5 4 3 2 1

First Edition: March 2014

Printed in the United States of America

To my dear Abba...who blessed me with the passion and the ability to write this book. Whatever benefit the reader obtains from the words that follow is entirely to His credit.

CONTENTS

Introduction   i

PART I: How did we get here?

QUESTION 1: Where did our educational system come from and what was its purpose?   3

PART II: How are we doing?

QUESTION 2: How did this book come about?   45

QUESTION 3: How well have compulsory government schools addressed the acquisition of knowledge?   47

QUESTION 4: The implications of "A Nation At Risk" are truly horrifying, but certainly government schooling in America has improved since 1983. Right?   49

QUESTION 5: Admittedly, our NAEP and SAT scores are absolutely terrible, but that is only because our national academic standards are so rigorous. Certainly, we compare more favorably against the rest of the world. Right?   53

QUESTION 6: Even though our NAEP, SAT, PISA, PIRLS, and TIMSS scores are consistently below mediocre, at least our literacy rates are among the highest in the world. Right?   57

QUESTION 7: Even though our NAEP, SAT, PISA, PIRLS, TIMSS scores, and literacy rates are perilously substandard, the only reason that U.S. students are lagging so far behind their international peers is because the federal government doesn't spend enough money on the problem. Right? — 59

QUESTION 8: Since the federal government spends so lavishly on public schooling, state governments must be to blame for not contributing enough money. Right? — 61

QUESTION 9: But since not all states spend the same amount of money on education, the five states spending the most money must be producing the best results. Right? — 63

QUESTION 10: If the federal and state governments are spending so much money to produce such abysmal results, then the fault must lie with local school districts who are under-spending on education. Right? — 67

QUESTION 11: Even if the LAUSD squandered most of their $7.3 billion budget, at least the money made a positive difference for their students. Right? — 71

QUESTION 12: If—according to their own metrics—compulsory government schooling is an abject failure and a colossal waste of money, then what exactly are educrats doing to improve it? — 73

QUESTION 13: Since the money that compulsory government schools spend is going somewhere, educrats must be spending it to educate, train, and hire the best teachers. Right? — 77

QUESTION 14: So, if "every profession has its failures", then how many bad teachers are there compared to other professions?   79

QUESTION 15: Why do teachers have such dramatically higher employee retention rates compared to other professions?   83

QUESTION 16: How do teachers themselves view tenure?   87

QUESTION 17: Even though educrats and teachers alike admit that other teachers are substandard, at least they still send *their own* children to government schools. Right?   89

QUESTION 18: Given the comprehensive failure of compulsory government schooling, why hasn't Congress done something to constructively address these obvious problems?   91

QUESTION 19: Just what exactly did that $543 million (2014 USD) buy?   97

QUESTION 20: Even though educrats have wasted… er…invested vast sums of money to "educate" primary and secondary school students, at least they've been prepared for college. Right?   99

QUESTION 21: What explains this collective absence of academic preparedness?   103

QUESTION 22: After these academically unprepared products of media immersion are enrolled in college, what are they doing with their time?   105

QUESTION 23: Even if these students are not using their time studying, they must be learning something in their classes. Right? — 107

QUESTION 24: So what is the explanation for this astonishing lack of basic civic knowledge? — 117

QUESTION 25: If these students aren't taking core general education courses, then what classes are they attending? — 119

QUESTION 26: Even if the majority of classes these students take are silly electives, at least they learned something after six years of college. Right? — 121

QUESTION 27: The ISI (2008) survey must have asked some pretty obscure questions for educated people to produce such poor results. Right? — 123

QUESTION 28: If these academically unprepared products of media immersion did not study, wasted their time taking silly electives, and their college degree failed to improve their "civic literacy"…then how do you explain the high GPA's of these graduates? — 125

QUESTION 29: Grade inflation, though certainly alarming, cannot completely explain the scandalous decline in educational standards. So, what else could it be? — 131

QUESTION 30: Why go to college if grade inflation, cheating, and administrative corruption have become so rampant? — 137

QUESTION 31: Even though the current cohort of America's college graduates are looking at mediocre in the rear-view mirror, at least they're doing better than previous generations. Right? — 139

QUESTION 32: Is the reason that students are substandard in basic skills like reading and writing because so many of them graduate with academic deficiencies and mediocre literacy rates? 143

QUESTION 33: What happens when these college graduates enter the marketplace? 147

QUESTION 34: Since we can look forward to being governed by substandard leaders, how will large-scale educational ignorance—and the academic dishonesty that supports it—affect our country? 155

QUESTION 35: Why does "higher education" cost so much money when it produces such poor results? 163

QUESTION 36: So, what exactly does a college degree do for you? 167

QUESTION 37: How does "education" ultimately impact our nation's civic values? 171

QUESTION 38: What should the purpose of education be? 173

Acknowledgments 177

About The Author 179

INTRODUCTION

Many Americans are becoming interested in what the U.S. Constitution actually says for perhaps the first time in their lives. But with this renewed civic curiosity comes the realization that we should have probably paid closer attention in the U.S. History, Government, and Economics classes that we attended in high school or college.

But those classes are the least of our national worries as we wrestle with the sobering question of how to preserve the legacy of "life, liberty, and the pursuit of happiness" the Framers bequeathed to us over 230 years ago.

The information in this book represents an important step towards reclaiming that fading legacy for our children.

After all, we are older now and have adult responsibilities like raising kids and paying bills. Sure, we could take a few online classes, but we have to make the mortgage payment instead. Besides, even if we had the money, who has the time? Someone's got to drive the kids to soccer practice and help with their homework.

Americans of the 1800's were similarly interested in the history and preservation of our nation, but few had the opportunity to pursue higher education. Into this academic void stepped the "lyceum movement" to bolster the development of adult education in America. These associations were varied and informal in nature, but generally served to improve the intellectual, social, and moral fabric of society.

The lyceum movement—through lectures, dramatic performances, class instructions, and debates—contributed significantly to the educational foundation of 19th century America. Noted lecturers, entertainers, and readers often traveled the "lyceum circuit," from town-to-town and state-to-state to speak, entertain, or debate for the benefit of their eager audiences.

If our nation is to endure, we must restore the spirit of this movement to correct the systemic deficiencies of the present educational structure—a lyceum 2.0 if you will. It was this spirit that empowered parents to confidently make *intentional choices* concerning their children's education.

Unfortunately, not everyone has the option to escape the public-school system, but for those who do, there are any number of wonderful alternatives: *homeschooling, private schools, charter schools, hybrid schools, apprenticeships, mentorships, co-ops, private tutoring, virtual/online education, et. al.*

However, before we go any further, allow me to explain what this book is *not*. It's not an "end-all-be-all" informational compendium. It's not the next *New York Times* bestseller (though I certainly wouldn't complain if it was). It's not destined for a place in the pantheon of literary greatness, and to be perfectly honest…several authors have already produced works far more comprehensive than my own.

Instead, consider this book an easy-to-absorb, well-researched introductory primer that will fill in the important gaps left behind from your high school or college years.

So why did I write this book?

Because I believe whole-heartedly in Thomas Jefferson's proposition that, "If a nation expects to be ignorant and free in a state of civilization, it expects what never was and never will be. If we are to guard against ignorance and remain free, it is the responsibility of every American to be informed."

Considering how comprehensively under-educated the students of our public-school system have become, his words have proven a tragically prescient indictment. In fact, the system has failed (by design) to truly educate us…and consequently our nation has grown *unnecessarily ignorant*, NOT stupid.

Since compulsory government schooling has become the primary "lens" through which society views our entire culture, this ignorance will prove utterly devastating unless it is reversed.

This lens is especially focused upon the four foundational "pillars" of American society: education, religion, economics, and politics…with education being the lens through which we most often view the other three.

It is therefore essential that every parent carefully consider the following questions concerning compulsory government schooling:

1. What is its purpose?
2. What results has produced?
3. How has its purpose and its results influenced our view of everything else?

We can no longer afford to be intellectually disengaged because if we forget what made this country so remarkable, the desire to preserve its legacy will dissipate as well.

Ronald Reagan (1911-2004), perhaps expressed this sentiment best when he said,

> "Freedom is never more than one generation away from extinction. We didn't pass it to our children in the bloodstream. It must be fought for, protected, and handed on for them to do the same, or one day we will spend our sunset years telling our children and our children's children what it was once like in the United States where men were free."

The practical intention of this book is to inspire *thinking-into-action* by placing a *maximum of information* into a *minimum of space* as *accessibly as possible*.

…For those who "just want the facts", this book is replete with concise selections of useful, heavily footnoted data with which to analyze the state of education in America and make informed choices.

…For those who are too busy enjoying life to devote countless hours to tedious research, this book does the work for you and will help you make informed choices.

…For those who just want to make a difference and improve the lives of others by offering them the data they need to make informed choices, this book will give you that information.

…For those who are tired of being told that someone else knows how to run your life better than you do, this book will enable you to "stay ahead of the curve" and empower you to make informed choices.

You may have noticed the "informed choices" theme. If you get nothing else from this book, you will become better informed than when you first picked it up.

However, as you continue the journey of self-education beyond these pages, I strongly encourage you to **ALWAYS** ask yourself four questions:

1. What do "they" mean by that?
2. How do "they" know it is true?
3. Where did "they" get their information?
4. What happens if "they" are wrong?

After all, if you don't think for yourself, someone else will always be happy to think for you.

PART I
How did we get here?

PART I: How did we get here?

QUESTION 1

Where did our educational system come from and what was its purpose?

"A nation of well informed men who have been taught to know and prize the rights which God has given them cannot be enslaved. It is in the region of ignorance that tyranny begins."
—BENJAMIN FRANKLIN (1706-1790)

"The only time my education was interrupted was when I was in school [...] My schooling not only failed to teach me what it professed to be teaching, but prevented me from being educated to an extent which infuriates me when I think of all I might have learned at home by myself."
—GEORGE BERNARD SHAW (1856-1950)

"Those who know how to think need no teachers."
—MOHANDAS GANDHI (1869-1948)

NOTE: Each of the following books offers a thorough, if disturbing, examination of why and how our compulsory government school system was established.

To fully understand the origins and purposes of this system, there is no better source of insight than John Taylor Gatto's[1] brilliantly researched musings—*Dumbing Us Down: The Hidden Curriculum of Compulsory Schooling (1991)*; *The Underground History of American Education (2003)*; *Weapons of Mass*

---

[1] Teacher of the Year: New York City (1989, 1990, 1991) and New York State (1991).

Instruction: A Schoolteacher's Journey Through the Dark World of Compulsory Schooling (2009)...or **Charlotte Thomson Iserbyt's**[2] **meticulously documented,** *The Deliberate Dumbing Down of America: A Chronological Paper Trail (1999)*...or **Samuel L. Blumenfeld's**[3] **insightful treatises,** *N.E.A.: Trojan Horse in American Education (1984), Is Public Education Necessary? (1985), New Illiterates and How You Can Keep Your Child from Becoming One (1988),* **and** *The Whole Language/OBE Fraud (1995).* **All are excellent resources.**

After fourteen years of teaching high school, both public and private, and speaking at numerous education conferences, I discovered that every audience shared a common desire (usually unspoken) to move beyond pre-packaged talking points and bumper-sticker rhetoric.

They. Just. Wanted. Real. Information.

So...try to recall whatever you can remember from your years of compulsory government schooling. How much value do you place on whatever you "learned" there?

Every year, I invited my students to answer precisely the same question. Their response? School is boring, mostly a waste of time, and they considered about 20% of what they learned there, "important."

My students were right. Schooling *is* largely a catastrophic waste of time. Especially considering that studies have proven the key to success in any field is—to a large extent—a matter of

---

2 Senior Policy Advisor in the Office of Educational Research and Improvement (OERI), U.S. Department of Education, during the first term of U.S. President Ronald Reagan, and staff employee of the U.S. Department of State (South Africa, Belgium, South Korea).
3 Internationally recognized leader in the systematic phonics movement.

practicing/studying a specific task for about 10,000 hours.[4]

So, after spending 18,200 hours being schooled (K-12), what did that time prepare you for? What doors of success[5] has that 18,200-hour "key" opened for you? And if all those hours failed to help you develop your fullest potential, then *what exactly was the purpose of school*? You might not like the answer.

The story actually begins with the ideas of Greek and Enlightenment philosophers➡ who influenced Prussia's educrats (education + bureaucrats)➡ whose prescriptions were later embraced by America's "Founding Fathers" of compulsory government schooling➡ which they faithfully transmitted to their disciples and to like-minded organizations.

Thus, the notion of establishing a utopic system of centralized schooling to train an elite ruling class capable of directing the masses (for their own good of course) is not exactly a new idea.

The following non-exhaustive sampling of quotes will provide a brief glimpse into the dark purposes of compulsory government schooling. Carefully consider the ideas that are expressed in the speaker's own words in order to formulate your own answer to the question, "What is the purpose of school?"

It all started with Plato…

Plato (424-348 BC) | *The Republic*: believed that enlightened philosopher-kings [the "Guardians"] should assign appropriate roles to citizens in order to serve the collective society. In this utopian State, the majority of the populace would be trained to

---

4 Malcolm Gladwell, *Outliers: The Story of Success* (New York, NY: Little, Brown & Company, 2008), citing the "10,000-Hour Rule."
5 Although the definition of professional success is very personal, it might be helpful for the reader to know mine…earning a living through the exercise of your individual passions and skills.

become obedient servants or soldiers, since only the "Guardians" were deemed worthy of being educated as independent thinkers.

> "...neither cities nor States nor individuals will ever attain perfection until the **small class of philosophers** whom we termed useless but not corrupt are providentially compelled, whether they will or not, to **take care of the State**, and until a like necessity be laid on the State to **obey them**..."[6]

Niccolò Machiavelli (1469-1527) | *The Prince*: believed that the elite were opinion-makers who exercised "adjustable virtue" in order to achieve their desired outcomes.

> "...they do not realise that in every republic there are **two different dispositions, that of the people and that of the great men**, and that all legislation favouring liberty is brought about by their dissension."[7]

Thomas Hobbes (1588-1679) | *The Leviathan*: asserted that everyone—except the sovereign [or State]—should renounce their familial rights and promise to devote their energies in service to the decisions of the sovereign.

> "[According to Hobbes]...social order depended upon state control of the inner life...without compulsory universal schooling the idiosyncratic family would never surrender its central hold on society to allow utopia to become reality. **Family had to be discouraged from its function as a sentimental haven**, pressed into the service of loftier ideals—those of the perfected State."[8]

---

6 *The Republic*, Book VI.
7 http://plato.stanford.edu/entries/machiavelli/.
8 John Taylor Gatto, *The Underground History of American Education* (New York, NY: Oxford Village Press, 2000).

Johann Gottlieb Fichte (1762-1814), the "Father of German Nationalism" and one of the founding figures of German Idealism, synthesized these concepts into an appalling philosophy of how students should be "taught":

> "If you want to influence the student at all, you must do more than merely talk to him; you must fashion him, and **fashion him in such a way that he simply cannot will otherwise than you wish him to will.**"[9]

And how to effectively crush the spirit of independent thinking:

> "**Education should aim at destroying free will** so that after pupils are thus schooled, they will be **incapable throughout the rest of their lives of thinking or acting otherwise than as their school masters would have wished**... The social psychologist of the future will have a number of classes of school children on whom they will try different methods of producing an unshakable conviction that snow is black. When the technique has been perfected, **every government that has been in charge of education for more than one generation will be able to control its subjects securely without the need of armies or policemen.**"[10]

Though ideological inspiration came from these and other philosophers, the practical impetus behind the efforts of Prussia's edutocracy (leading families + heads of academic institutions) actually began with Napoleon's victory over Prussia at the Battles of Saalfeld, Jena, and Auerstedt in 1806.

---

9 Johann Gottlieb Fichte, *Addresses to the German Nation*, "Second Address: The General Nature of the New Education", trans. R. F. Jones & G. H. Turnbull, (Chicago, IL & London, UK: The Open Court Publishing Company, 1922), p. 21.
10 Bertrand Russell, *The Impact of Science on Society* (New York, NY: Routledge, 1952), quoting Johann Gottlieb Fichte.

In the aftermath of defeat, Prussia became convinced that the independent thinking of their soldiers on the battlefield had ensured the Frenchman's victory.

To prevent this from ever happening again, Prussian educrats established a compulsory three-tiered school system (c.1819), with five principal goals:[11]

1) Create obedient soldiers for the army.
2) Create obedient workers for the factories and mines.
3) Create well-subordinated civil servants for the government.
4) Create well-subordinated clerks for industry.
5) Create citizens who share a national consensus on major issues.

The Prussian edutocracy believed that schools were the perfect instrument to accomplish these goals and forge a national consensus on matters that had been pre-decided by the elites.

In order to achieve this, educrats developed a system that divided the population into three tiers:

❑ 0.5% of the population was taught to think and attended the *Akademiensschulen*.[12] They "learned to think strategically, contextually, in wholes; they learned complex processes, and useful knowledge, studied history, wrote copiously, argued often, read deeply, and mastered tasks of command."

They would become Prussia's policy makers.

---

11 John Taylor Gatto, "Origins & History of American Compulsory Schooling", interview with Jim Martin, *Flatland Magazine*, No. 11.
12 Gatto simplified this tripartite division to clarify its functional logic. In some places, the "academy" portion was represented as a division within the *Realsschulen* (e.g. similar to today's "gifted", "honors", "advanced placement", and "international baccalaureate" programs).

❏ 5.5% to 7.5% of the population was taught to partially think and attended the *Realsschulen*. They were "intended mostly as a manufactory for the professional proletariat of engineers, architects, doctors, lawyers, career civil servants, and such other assistants as policy thinkers at times would require. Their learning acquired a superficial capacity to think in context, but was mostly applied to managing 'materials, men, and situations—to be problem solvers.'"

This group would also staff the various policing functions of the State.

❏ 92 to 94% of the population was taught to reject independent thinking, to obey authority without question, to promote collective cooperation, and attended the *Volksschulen*. They would become the compliant masses that served the upper two tiers.

John Taylor Gatto described Prussia's educratic vision this way:

> "This particular utopia had a different target than human equality; it aimed instead for **frictionless efficiency**. From its inception *Volksschulen*, the 'people's place', **heavily discounted reading**; reading produced dissatisfaction, it was thought… Reading offered too many windows onto better lives, too much familiarity with better ways of thinking. It was a gift unwise to share with those permanently consigned to low station."[13]

In their efforts to produce "frictionless efficiency", Prussian educrats devised a system of schooling that separated the *Volksschulen's* curriculum into a series of sections.

---

13 John Taylor Gatto, *The Underground History of American Education* (New York, NY: Oxford Village Press, 2000).

First, it divided whole ideas (that naturally interconnected mathematics, science, social thinking, history, language, and art) into smaller unconnected subjects, most of which had barely existed before.

Then, it further divided these unconnected subjects into smaller units of time until no one understood what was actually happening.

Eventually, they established enough of these variations in the course of daily instruction to condition their students into full compliance, ready to unquestioningly serve the directives of the edutocracy.

The ultimate purpose of this third-tier was to reduce both the classroom and the workplace into "simplified fragments that anyone, however dumb, can memorize and operate."

Thus, the historical dilemma of leadership was neatly solved.

"[A] disobedient work force could be replaced quickly, without damage to production, if the workers required only habit," not independent thought, "to function properly."

After all, if *anyone* can do *any* particular job, "there is no reason to pay them very much except to guarantee employee loyalty and dependency."

In this way, Prussia's educrats successfully codified the ideas of Plato, Hobbes, Machiavelli, and Fichte, et. al. into their system of compulsory government schooling.

The very same system that the "Founding Fathers of Public School"—Horace Mann, William Torrey Harris, G. Stanley Hall, John Dewey, Ellwood P. Cubberley, Edward L. Thorndike, Alexander J. Inglis, and James Bryant Conant, et. al.—slavishly admired and later brought to America.

When the Prussian school system finally landed on American shores, the sheer comprehensiveness of its systematized ideas and pre-determined outcomes was so overwhelming that students eventually abandoned any attempt at thinking for themselves.

By the 1890's, the educational philosophies of America's "Founding Fathers" of compulsory government schooling had successfully infected the entire public-school system.

In fact, they were so successful that their toxic ideas have now become part of our educational DNA and their malignant influence continues to be felt even to this very day.

After all, the effort to be creative, or to think independently makes little sense when schools and the media are offering thousands of pre-formulated ideas, opinions, facts, and "social consensus" to guide our collective moral compass.

These pre-formulated ideas were imbedded into the textbooks that I had the misfortune of *teaching* from during fourteen years in the classroom.

Despite the elitist, collectivist, statist, Darwinist, humanist progressivism of these "Founding Fathers", we must at least credit their honesty in describing their goals.

As you read the following selection of their thoughts and agendas, carefully consider the consequences for your children.

Horace Mann (1796-1859), graduate of Brown University; "Father of the Common School Movement", served in the MA House of Representatives, the MA Senate, the U.S. House of Representatives, and as Secretary of the MA State Board of Education. Later established (1) a compulsory school system in Massachusetts eventually adopted by the other states and (2) "normal schools" to train professional teachers.

In 1852, he advocated for the adoption of the Prussian school system in Massachusetts.

> "We who are engaged in the **sacred cause of education** are **entitled** to look upon all parents as having given **hostages** to our cause."[14]

William Torrey Harris (1835-1909), graduate of Yale University; served as superintendent of schools in St. Louis, MO, established America's first permanent public kindergarten (1873), founded and edited America's first philosophical periodical, the *Journal of Speculative Philosophy, (1867-1893)*, and was U.S. Commissioner of Education until 1906.

During his tenure as commissioner, he nearly succeeded in establishing Hegelianism [which stated all reality was capable of being expressed in rational categories] as the official philosophy of American education.

According to Harris, students should be kept in their places:

> "**Our schools have been scientifically designed to prevent over-education from happening.** The average American [should be] content with their humble role in life, because they're not tempted to think about any other role."[15]

In order to become properly standardized into predictability:

> "**Ninety-nine [students] out of a hundred are automata**, careful to walk in prescribed paths, careful to follow the prescribed custom.

---

14 Horace Mann, *Lectures and Annual Reports on Education* (Boston, MA: Lee & Shepard Publishers, 1872) "The Work of Education", p. 210.
15 John Taylor Gatto, *Dumbing Us Down: The Hidden Curriculum of Compulsory Schooling* (Philadelphia, PA: New Society Publishers, 1992).

> "This is not an accident, [but the] result of substantial education, which, scientifically defined, is the **subsumption of the individual.**"[16]

And these goals were best achieved in prison-like conditions:

> "**The great purposes of school can be realized better in dark, airless, ugly places than in beautiful halls.** It is to master the physical self, to transcend the beauty of nature. School should develop the power to withdraw from the external world."[17]

G. Stanley Hall (1844-1924), graduate of Harvard University; psychologist whose research focused on childhood development and evolutionary theory, served as professor of psychology and pedagogics at Johns Hopkins University (1882-1888), founded the *American Journal of Psychology (1887)*, and was the first president of Clark University (1889-1920).

He was also John Dewey's personal mentor at Johns Hopkins University.

Hall altered the basic structure of schooling in America and his legacy included (1) "[being] *the man who gave us 'adolescence' and doomed generations of otherwise capable teenagers to perpetual childhood*"[18] and (2) the then-unprecedented age-segregated classroom.

---

16 Cf. Derrick Jensen, *Walking on Water: Reading, Writing, and Revolution* (White River Junction, VT: Chelsea Green Publishing Company, 2004), p. 37.
17 John Taylor Gatto, *Dumbing Us Down* (Philadelphia, PA: New Society Publishers, 1992).
18 Howard P. Chudacoff, *How Old Are You? Age Consciousness in American Culture* (Princeton, NJ: Princeton University Press, 1989), pp. 66-67; cf. Otto Scott, "The Invention of Adolescence", *Chalcedon Report* (July 1991); G. Stanley Hall, *Adolescence: Its Psychology and Its Relations to Physiology, Anthropology, Sociology, Sex, Crime, Religion and Education, Vols. I & II*, (New York, NY: D. Appleton & Company, 1904).

(Age-segregation is completely foreign to real life where one must interact with people of all ages in a variety of settings).

In promoting national standardized testing, Hall shrewdly brought Sigmund Freud to the United States to "legitimize" his theory that behavioral problems in later life could be *directly linked to deficient parenting*...and thus *only alleviated by the interventions of educrats*.

Freud's deeply flawed theories would later find wide acceptance among the leadership of the National Education Association (NEA).

This de-emphasis on thinking might explain why Hall later admonished, "Reading should no longer be a fetish. Little attention should be paid to reading." After all, readers become thinkers and educrats certainly did not want that to happen.

John Dewey (1859-1952), graduate of Johns Hopkins University; "Father of Modern Public Education", influential philosopher, psychologist, and educational reformer whose principal works include, *My Pedagogic Creed (1897), The School and Society (1900), The Child and the Curriculum (1902), Democracy and Education (1916),* **and** *Experience and Education (1938).*

Allowing people—other than his fellow educrats—to think for themselves was...well...unthinkable for Dewey:

> "...independent, self-reliant people would be a **counterproductive anachronism** in the collective society of the future. In modern society, **people would be defined by their associations**—the group to which they belonged—not by their own individual accomplishments."[19]

---

19 John Taylor Gatto, "Our Prussian School System", Cato Policy Report 15, No. 2 (March/April 1993).

> "**The children who know how to think for themselves, spoil the harmony of the collective society** which is coming, where everyone would be interdependent."[20]

Dewey's *My Pedagogic Creed (1897)*, offered a chilling insight into his designs for government schooling:

> "The only true education comes through the stimulation of the child's powers by the demands of the social situation in which he finds himself. Through these demands, he is stimulated to act as a member of a unity, to emerge from his original narrowness of action and feeling, and to **conceive of himself from the standpoint of the welfare of the group to which he belongs...**"[21]

And the "curriculum" and "purpose" that he believed should be taught in those schools:

> "The true center of correlation on the school subjects is not science, nor literature, nor history, nor geography, but the child's own social activities..."[22]

> "I believe that the school is primarily a social institution... Examinations are of use only so far as they test the child's fitness for social life..."[23]

---

20 John Taylor Gatto, "The Tyranny of Government Schooling" (1992).
21 John Dewey, *The Essential Dewey: Pragmatism, education, democracy, Vol. 1*, eds. Larry A. Hickman & Thomas M. Alexander (Bloomington, IN: Indiana University Press, 1998), p. 229. Citing *My Pedagogic Creed* (1897).
22 John Dewey, *The Essential Dewey: Pragmatism, education, democracy, Vol. 1*, eds. Larry A. Hickman & Thomas M. Alexander (Bloomington, IN: Indiana University Press, 1998), p. 232. Citing *My Pedagogic Creed* (1897).
23 Cited in Dennis L. Cuddy, Ph.D., *Chronology of Education With Quotable Quotes* (Highland City, FL: Pro Family Forum, Inc., 1993), p. 9.

And the role of teachers in proselytizing these ideas:

> "Every teacher should realize he is a social servant set apart for the maintenance of the proper social order and the securing of the right social growth. **In this way the teacher is always the prophet of the true God and the usherer in of the true kingdom of heaven.**"[24]

[*Since Dewey was a devout atheist, his frequent use of religious metaphors is quite ironic.*][25]

The submission of the individual to the collective propelled the edutocracy's crusade to transform schooling. In fact, Dewey's *Democracy and Education (1916)*, literally equated individualism with insanity:

> "There is always a danger that **increased personal independence will decrease the social capacity of an individual...** It often makes an individual so insensitive in his relations to others as to develop an illusion of being really able to stand and act alone—**an unnamed form of insanity** which is responsible for a large part of the remedial suffering of the world."[26]

In 1930, when Dewey retired as professor of philosophy at both Columbia University and Columbia University's Teachers College, he passed the torch to his beloved disciples...Drs. **George S. Counts (1889-1974)** and **Harold O. Rugg (1886-1960)**.

---

[24] John Dewey, *My Pedagogic Creed* (New York, NY: E. L. Kellogg & Company, 1897).

[25] Cf. Ralph A. Epperson, *The New World Order* (Tucson, AZ: Publius Press, 1990). "There is no god, and there is no soul. There are no needs for the props of traditional religion... With dogma and creed excluded, then immutable truth is also dead and buried... There is no room for fixed, natural law or permanent moral absolutes."

[26] Cited in Dennis L. Cuddy, Ph.D., *Chronology of Education With Quotable Quotes* (Highland City, FL: Pro Family Forum, Inc., 1993), p. 13.

Dr. Rugg, President of the American Educational Research Association and author of fourteen social studies textbooks, said in *The Great Technology (1933)*:

> "Education must be used to **condition the people** to accept social change… **The chief function of schools is to plan the future of society.**"[27]

John Taylor Gatto described Rugg's ultimate objectives this way:

> "Rugg advocated that the major task of schools be seen as **'indoctrinating' youth**, using social 'science' as the 'core of the school curriculum' to bring about **the desired climate of public opinion.**"[28]

Unsurprisingly, Dr. Counts agreed with Dr. Rugg's conclusions, and even admitted to Dewey:

> "You will say, no doubt, that I am flirting with the idea of **indoctrination**. And my answer is again in the affirmative, or, at least, I should say that the **word does not frighten me.**"[29]

Counts believed this comprehensive indoctrination could be accomplished:

> "…in school activities, in the relations of pupils and teachers and administrators, the ideal of a cooperative commonwealth should prevail…

---

[27] Harold O. Rugg, *The Great Technology: Social Chaos and the Public Mind* (New York, NY: The John Day Company, 1933).
[28] Quoted in John Taylor Gatto, *The Underground History of American Education* (New York, NY: Oxford Village Press, 2000).
[29] George S. Counts, "Dare Progressive Education Be Progressive?", *Progressive Education*, Vol. 9 (1932), p. 263.

"All of this applies quite as strictly to the **nursery, the kindergarten, and the elementary school** as to the **secondary school, the college, and the university.**"[30]

In *Crowd Culture (1952)*, Dr. Bernard Bell explained the goals of Dewey's disciples in this way:

"To the Dewyites, a sound education is one which **accustoms the pupils to discover group convictions and then conform to them**. This is known as 'becoming socially adjusted'... they assume that...**the group is always more trustworthy and wise than anyone within it.**"[31]

In 1960, Lewis A. Alesen, M.D., President of the California Medical Association, perceptively described the consequences of Dewey's educational philosophy:

"Thus, even at this early period in his teaching experience, John Dewey **emphasized the pre-dominance of the group over the individual**. To be sure, Professor Dewey may have borrowed from some of the muddled naturalism of Jean Jacques Rousseau (1712-1778); and he may have been influenced a bit by the teachings and practice of the Swiss pedagogue Johann Heinrich Pestalozzi (1746-1827); but **the particular brand he placed upon philosophy was his own...**

"Since, in terms of this philosophy, the chief end in life is the achievement of happiness by adjusting oneself to it...and, since there are **no fixed rules or basic truths of any value whatsoever**, the growing child is taught, day by day, that it is more important to get along with his fellows, that is, the

---

[30] George S. Counts, "A Call to the Teachers of the Nation", Progressive Education Association (U.S.), Committee on Social and Economic Problems (1933), p. 22.
[31] Cited in Dennis L. Cuddy, Ph.D., *Chronology of Education With Quotable Quotes* (Highland City, FL: Pro Family Forum, Inc., 1993), p. 29.

group, and to adjust himself to his environment, than it is to develop himself in any particular skills.

"Thus he is **encouraged to deny and reject responsibility for himself** from the very day he enters kindergarten all through his academic course, and to **transfer that responsibility to the group**...

"Since, in this view, there is no such entity as absolute truth, no possibility of immutable physical, mathematics, or moral law, **the progressive educator sees no use in wasting the student's time in studying history, because, of course, what other men have done and thought in the past is not of any particular value**, as the circumstances under which they lived were entirely different from those facing the student and citizen today.

"**Likewise, there is no point to the study of mathematics under this philosophy, which denies the existence of basic truths**..."[32]

It is worth noting that not everyone agreed with the ideas of these elitist educrats. In fact, they were widely unpopular with the American public, and prominent philosophers among both Dewey's predecessors and contemporaries were *staunchly pro-individualist*. Among those holding these opposing views were...

British philosopher **John Stuart Mill (1806-1873)**, who astutely warned of the dangers of anti-individualism:

"**A general State education is a mere contrivance for moulding people to be exactly like one another**; and as the mould in which it casts them is that which pleases the dominant power in the government, whether this be a monarch, an aristocracy, or a majority of the existing generation; in proportion as it is

---

32 Lewis A. Alesen, M.D., *Mental Robots* (Caldwell, ID: Caxton Printers, Ltd., 1960), p. 59-60.

efficient and successful, **it establishes a despotism over the mind,** leading by a natural tendency to one over the body."[33]

British writer **Rudyard Kipling (1865-1936)**, who likewise cautioned against anti-individualism:

"The individual has always had to struggle to keep from being overwhelmed by the tribe. To be your own man is hard business. If you try it, you will be lonely often, and sometimes frightened. **But no price is too high to pay for the privilege of owning yourself.**"[34]

Scottish writer **Sir Walter Scott (1771-1832)**, who identified a simple solution to repairing the sort of utopic anti-individualism later envisioned by Dewey, et. al.:

"All men who have turned out worth anything have had the chief hand in **their own education.**"[35]

Unfortunately, the views of these men prevailed instead…

Ellwood P. Cubberley (1868-1941), graduate of Columbia University; pioneered the field of educational administration, served as Dean of Education at the Stanford University School of Education, and authored *Syllabus of Lectures on the History of Education (1902)*, *Changing Conceptions in Education (1909)*, *Public Education in the United States (1919)*, *The History of Education (1920)*, *Readings in the History of Education (1920)*, *A Brief History of Education (1922)*, **and** *Public School Administration (1929)*.

---

[33] John Stuart Mill, *On Liberty* (London, UK: Longman, Roberts & Green, 1869).
[34] *Reader's Digest* (1935). Reprinted in *Kipling Society Journal*, "Six Hours with Rudyard Kipling" (1967).
[35] *Ivanhoe* (1820).

Cubberley fervently believed in the power of the State to manufacture children according to its needs:

> "Only a system of state-controlled schools can be free to teach **whatever the welfare of the State may demand**."[36]

> "**Schools should serve as factories in which raw products, children, are to be shaped and formed into finished products...manufactured like nails**, and the specifications for manufacturing will come from government and industry."[37]

Edward L. Thorndike (1874-1949), graduate of Columbia University; "Father of Modern Educational Psychology", served as a board member of the Psychological Corporation, and was president of the American Psychological Association (1912).

While teaching at the Rockefeller-sponsored Columbia Teachers College Thorndike announced, "Academic subjects are of little value"[38] and went on to add:

> "Despite rapid progress in the right direction, the program of the average elementary school has been primarily devoted to teaching the fundamental subjects, the three R's, and closely related disciplines... **Subjects such as arithmetic, language, and history include content that is intrinsically of little value. Nearly every subject is enlarged unwisely** to satisfy the academic ideal of thoroughness... Elimination of the unessential by scientific study, then, is **one step in improving the curriculum.**"[39]

---

36 Ellwood Patterson Cubberley, *Public Education in the United States: A Study and Interpretation of American Educational History* (Cambridge, MA: The Riverside Press, 1919), p. 121.
37 Excerpted from his 1905 dissertation for Columbia Teachers College.
38 John Taylor Gatto, *Weapons of Mass Instruction* (Canada, BC: New Society Publishers, 2009), p. 2.
39 Edward L. Thorndike & Arthur I. Gates, *Elementary Principles of Education* (New York, NY: Macmillan, 1929).

According to Thorndike, teaching was defined as:

"The art of giving and withholding stimuli with the result of producing or preventing certain responses… **The aim of the teacher is to produce desirable and prevent undesirable changes in human beings by producing and preventing certain responses.**

"The means at the disposal of the teacher are…**the teacher's words, gestures, and appearance, the condition and appliances of the school room, the books to be used, and objects to be seen**, and so on through a long list of the things and events which the **teacher can control**."[40]

Considering the abundance of neurological research confirming a direct link between the brain's size and complexity and the intensity of thinking during early childhood…Thorndike's absurd conclusions are orbiting the distant side of planet Totally Wrong.

Alexander J. Inglis (1879-1924),[41] graduate of Wesleyan University; influential progressive-experimentalist, professor at Harvard University Teachers College, and advocate of the comprehensive high school during the early-20th century.

In *Weapons of Mass Instruction*, John Taylor Gatto vividly exposes the appalling intentions of Inglis and explains how modern, industrialized, compulsory schooling was designed to divide the "prospective unity" of the "underclasses."

Inglis argued that his "educational utopia" could be realized by systematically separating children according to age, subject, class rank, and test scores.

---

40 Edward L. Thorndike, *The Principles of Teaching Based on Psychology* (New York, NY: A. G. Seiler, 1925).
41 Alexander Inglis, *Principles of Secondary Education* (Cambridge, MA: The Riverside Press, 1918).

Once in place, these artificially constructed divisions would almost certainly prevent the masses from reintegrating into a society of [gasp] independent thinkers.

To that end, Inglis organized his true purpose for government schooling into six basic functions…*each of which should horrify anyone who reflexively swallows the edutocracy's self-serving hype*.

1) The adjustive or adaptive function. Schools must establish "fixed habits of reaction to authority." Naturally, critical thinking must be carefully avoided and "useful or interesting material" simply must not be taught.

After all, it is impossible to test for reflexive obedience until "you know whether you can make kids learn, and do, foolish and boring things."

2) The integrating function. This could also be termed "the conformity function" because its intention is to make children as alike as possible. People who conform "are predictable, and this quality is highly valued by those who wish to harness and manipulate a large labor force."

3) The diagnostic and directive function. School is designed to determine each student's proper social role. This is accomplished by "logging evidence mathematically and anecdotally on cumulative records." As in "your permanent record."

4) The differentiating function. Once schools have successfully "diagnosed" a child's social role, they are to be categorized by that role and trained only as far as their destination in the social machine merits—not one step further. *So much for helping children achieve their personal best*.

5) The selective function. This relies on applying Darwin's theory of natural selection to what he termed "the favored races."

Consequently, schools are required to intentionally improve the breeding stock by labeling the unfit "with poor grades, remedial placement, and other punishments—clearly enough that their peers will accept them as inferior" and effectively exclude them "from the reproductive sweep-stakes."

This is the real motivation behind the countless humiliations from first grade onward…"to wash the dirt down the drain."

6) **The propaedeutic function.** The social system created by applying these functions requires an elite group of "caretakers."

To fulfill that requirement, a small fraction of the children will be discreetly taught "how to manage this continuing project and how to watch over and control a population deliberately dumbed down and declawed."

Once equipped with this knowledge, the caretaker class will "allow government to proceed unchallenged and ensure that corporations will never lack an obedient pool of labor to draw from."

James Bryant Conant (1893-1978), graduate of Harvard University; developed poison gases for the U.S. Army during World War I, president of Harvard University, U.S. High Commissioner for Germany during the military occupation after 1945, and the first U.S. Ambassador to West Germany.

John Taylor Gatto credited Conant's, *The American High School Today (1959)*, as being the catalyst for dramatically increasing the size of secondary schools during the 1960s.

This was accomplished vis-à-vis the forced consolidation of several smaller school districts into larger ones.

Conant justified these unprecedented changes by claiming that [during the Cold War], "Only large schools, could have faculty and facilities large enough to cover the math and science we [presumably] lacked and Russia [presumably] had. The bigger the better…"

In Gatto's view,[42] Conant envisioned school as "a triumph of Anglo/Germanic pragmatism, a pinnacle of the social technocrat's problem-solving art." **It comprehensively limited the American entrepreneurial spirit,** "a mission undertaken on perfectly sensible grounds, at least from a management perspective."

After all, if "capital investments" remained at the disposal "of millions of self-reliant, resourceful young entrepreneurs", who would fund the exorbitant cost of tooling and re-tooling the "commercial/industrial/financial machine?"

As long as the entire population was given the opportunity to become potential producers, young entrepreneurs remained unpredictable and uncontrollable.

However, **once confined to "employee status" they could be mass-produced into a reliably predictable "domestic market."**

Another prominent Harvard University professor, Robert Ulich, echoed Conant's earlier sentiments in his own book, *Philosophy of Education (1961)*:

> "[We are producing] more and more people who will be dissatisfied because the **artificially prolonged time of formal schooling** will arouse in them hopes which society cannot fulfill…

---

42 John Taylor Gatto, *The Underground History of American Education* (New York, NY: Oxford Village Press, 2000).

"These men and women will form **the avant-garde of the disgruntled**. It is no exaggeration to say [people like these] were responsible for World War II."[43]

But it wasn't just the "Founding Fathers" who advocated for the transformation of our government school system...

In 1909, **Woodrow Wilson (1856-1924)**, then-president of Princeton University, addressed the New York City School Teachers Association:

> "We want one class to have a liberal education. We want another class, a very much larger class of necessity, **to forego the privilege of a liberal education** and fit themselves to perform specific difficult manual tasks."[44]

Wilson deviously avoided revealing to his audience of teachers that they were *not* included in "that class to have a liberal education."

Although the "tasks" of teachers would not be physical, they would be as carefully prescribed as any factory workers. Just like the immigrants they were responsible for dumbing down; teachers were likewise being equipped to fulfill their "proper role in society."

On the other hand, traditional one-room schools, which had been successfully operated by locals with the express purpose of raising independent, responsible farmers who could run their own affairs...*were unable to meet this demand for standardization.*

---

43 Cf. John Taylor Gatto, *The Underground History of American Education* (New York, NY: Oxford Village Press, 2000).
44 Association of American Colleges & Universities. http://www.aacu.org/liberaleducation/le-su09/le-su09_president.cfm. Accessed 12 August 2012.

Since the industrial economy of that era required millions of laborers willing to mindlessly follow orders, an explanation for the wide-open immigration policies of 1909 becomes self-evident.

Converting desperate immigrants into interchangeable industrial workers was far easier than reshaping independent farmers "ruined" by years of self-reliance and social responsibility.

After all, the edutocracy certainly didn't want workers educated in the patriotism of Washington, Jefferson, and Adams…which viewed America as a country worthy to be preserved.

And mathematics? Reading? Writing? Science? History?

Seriously? The more dumbed down the better.

Remember the words of Wilson concerning those "fitted to perform specific difficult manual tasks" who required only a minimalistic, dumbed-down version of these "basics."

Sadly, to this day, students from across the nation can graduate from the Woodrow Wilson High Schools of America with honors, with AP/IB credits, with excellent SAT/ACT scores…*and still have to enroll in remedial college classes*.

[SIDENOTE: According to *The Hechinger Report*, data from 911 two- and four-year colleges revealed that *96% of schools enrolled students who required remediation in the 2014-15 academic year*. At least *209 of those schools placed more than half of incoming students* in at least one remedial course].

In 1914, eminent University of Wisconsin sociologist **Edward A. Ross (1866-1951)**, and a favorite of President Theodore Roosevelt, stated with appalling candor:

"The role of **the public official**, and in particular of **the public school teacher**, is to collect little **plastic lumps of human dough** from private households and **shape them on the social kneading board**."[45]

Since compulsory government schools were widely viewed as laboratories for behavioral psychology experiments, another advocate of this "transformation" was sociologist **B. F. Skinner (1904-1990)**.

In his seminal work, *Walden Two (1948)*, Skinner advanced the necessity of developing an entirely new paradigm of humanity:

"What was needed was a **new conception of man**, compatible with our scientific knowledge."[46]

He later outlined the practical steps to achieving this "new conception of man" in *Science and Human Behavior (1953)*:

"Operant **conditioning shapes behavior** as a sculptor shapes a lump of clay."

Sounds like Skinner was simply channeling the twisted spirit of Edward A. Ross, doesn't it?

Another influential figure of the "transformation" was educational psychologist **Dr. Benjamin Bloom (1913-1999)**, "the Father of Outcome-based Education."

---

45 Edward Alsworth Ross, *Social Control: A survey of the foundations of order* (New York, NY: The Macmillan Co., 1901). Cited in Paul C. Violas, "Progressive Social Philosophy: Charles Horton Cooley and Edward Alsworth Ross," in C. J. Karier, P. C. Violas, & J. Spring, eds., *Roots of Crisis: American Education in the 20th Century* (Chicago, IL: Rand McNally, 1973), pp. 40-65.
46 Charlotte Iserbyt, *The Deliberate Dumbing Down of America* (Ravenna, OH: Conscience Press, 1999), pp. 40, 48.

In 1956, he published *Taxonomy of Educational Objectives: The Classification of Educational Goals*, in which he explained the objectives of quality teaching:

> "...**a student attains 'higher order thinking' when he no longer believes in right or wrong**... A large part of what we call good teaching is a teacher's ability to obtain affective objectives by **challenging the student's fixed beliefs**...a large part of what we call teaching is that **the teacher should be able to use education to reorganize a child's thoughts, attitudes, and feelings**."[47]

Later, Bloom published, *All Our Children Learning (1981)* in which he clarified, "*the purpose of education and the schools is to change the thoughts, feelings and actions of students.*"[48]

Most of us would agree that a basic foundation of factual knowledge should anchor all meaningful thinking processes.

However, Bloom's model (1) relegated *factual* knowledge and *comprehension* to the ranks of *lower order thinking skills*, (2) suggested that *traditional knowledge* had become *largely insignificant and possibly even a hindrance to learning*, and (3) elevated the more *subjective* processes (e.g., evaluation, analysis, synthesis, and application) to *higher order thinking skills*.

Consequently, Bloom's theories failed to explain how students could evaluate, analyze, synthesize, and apply...*without facts*. Or how they could they arrive at rational conclusions...*without comprehension*.

---

47 Benjamin Bloom, ed., *Taxonomy of Educational Objectives, Vol. I*, "Major Categories in the Taxonomy of Educational Objectives" (New York, NY: David O. McKay, 1956), p. 185.
48 Benjamin Bloom, *All Our Children Learning* (New York, NY: McGraw Hill Paperbacks, 1981), pp. 33, 35.

This would be like attempting to write complete sentences and paragraphs without first memorizing the alphabet or rules of grammar. Absent foundational facts or comprehension, "higher order thinking skills" can *only* lead to *subjective, uncertain, and superficial* answers.

In fact, parents would be stunned to discover how easily *"biased information, carefully designed hypothetical stories, and pointed Socratic questioning"*, can be employed to persuade children that their personal beliefs and values are incompatible with modern 21st century society.

It's quite revealing that Bloom's *Taxonomy* still enjoys wide acceptance and devotion among administrators, teachers, and schools of teacher education.

This almost certainly explains the edutocracy's obsession with "conditioning" children…

In 1962, the National Institute of Mental Health (NIMH) published a report reiterating the importance of educational conditioning:

> "Education does not mean teaching people to know what they do not know…it means **teaching them to behave as they do not behave.**"[49]

But it gets even worse. The edutocracy accuses *parents of being part of the problem*!

In 1973, Chester M. Pierce, M.D., Professor of Education and Psychiatry at Harvard University addressed the Childhood International Education Seminar in Boulder, CO:

---

[49] National Institute of Mental Health (NIMH), "The Role of Schools in Mental Health" (1962). Cited in John Taylor Gatto, *The Underground History of American Education* (New York, NY: Oxford Village Press, 2000), Chapter 13.

> "Every child in America entering school at the age of five **is mentally ill** because he comes to school with certain allegiances to our founding fathers, toward our elected officials, toward his parents, toward a belief in a supernatural being, and toward the sovereignty of this nation as a separate entity. **It's up to you as teachers to make all these sick children well by creating the international child of the future.**"[50]

In 1979, the Association of California School Administrators *directly identified parental choice as THE problem*:

> "'Parent choice' proceeds from the belief that the purpose of education is to provide individual students with an education. In fact, **educating the individual is but a means to the true end of education**, which is to **create a viable social order** to which individuals contribute and by which they are sustained."[51]

In 1996, the U.S. Department of Education's Office of Educational Research & Improvement reported:

> "**Parent's attitudes** about what they want for their children represent one of **the greatest barriers** to successful implementation of school-to-work."[52]

Perhaps that's why educrats feel smugly justified in demanding that parent's step aside and leave child-rearing to the "experts"...

In 2008, Melissa Harris-Perry, MSNBC host and professor of political science at Tulane University (she formerly taught at the University of Chicago and Princeton University) remarked:

---

50 John Taylor Gatto, *The Underground History of American Education*, Chapter 13.
51 Cited in Ray C. Rist, ed., *Policy Issues for the 1990s, Vol. 9*, p. 738.
52 Ray Ryan & Susan Imel, "School-to-Work Transition: Genuine Reform or the Latest Fad?" *THE ERIC REVIEW*, Vol. 4, No. 2 (Spring 1996), p. 7.

"We have never invested as much in public education as we should have. Because of all, we have kind of a private notion of children. Your kid is yours and totally your responsibility. **We haven't had a very collective notion of these are our children.**

"So part of it is we have to **break through our kind of private idea that kids belong to their parents or kids belong to their families** and recognize that **kids belong to whole communities.** Once it's **everybody's responsibility** and not just the households then we start making better investments."[53]

Ultimately, educrats have become collectively convinced that their version of educational utopia is being thwarted by:

1. Anyone trying to think for themselves [the elite know how to live your life better than you do] and…

2. Parents who want to raise their own children according to their own values [gasp].

Irrespective of your religious convictions (or non-religious convictions), ALL parents should be profoundly disturbed that *tax-payer funded compulsory government schools* **presume to teach religion to their children.**

The teaching of religious or non-religious values is deeply personal and should be exclusively reserved to the parent. It is therefore rather curious that John Dewey and his fellow acolytes *often express their objectives in explicitly religious terms*.

Charles F. Potter (1885-1962), adviser to Clarence Darrow during the Scopes Trial (1925); founded the First Humanist Society of New York (1929) whose advisory board included Julian Huxley, John Dewey, Albert Einstein, and Thomas Mann; one of the

---

53 http://dailycaller.com/2013/04/08/msnbcs-melissa-harris-perry-wants-your-children/.

original 34 signatories (incl. Dewey) of the *Humanist Manifesto I (1933)*; and founder of the Euthanasia Society of America (1938).

Potter vehemently argued in favor of *using education to proselytize humanism* in the classroom:

> "**Education is thus a most powerful ally of humanism, and every American school is a school of humanism.** What can a theistic Sunday school's meeting for an hour once a week and teaching only a fraction of the children do to stem the tide of the **five-day program of humanistic teaching**?"[54]

Influential humanist John J. Dunphy stated the purpose of the humanist religion this way:

> "I am convinced that **the battle for humankind's future must be waged and won in the public school classroom** by teachers that correctly **perceive their role as proselytizers of a new faith**: a religion of humanity that recognizes and respects the spark of what theologian's call divinity in every human being...
>
> "The classroom must and will become an arena of conflict between the old and new—the rotting corpse of Christianity, together with all its adjacent evils and misery, and **the new faith of humanism...**"[55]

Contrary to popular opinion, our system of compulsory government schooling actively promotes religion...the religion of Secular Humanism. And yes, it is a religion according to the U.S. Supreme Court ruling in *Torcaso v. Watkins, 367 U.S. 488 (1961)*:

---

54 Charles Francis Potter, *Humanism: A New Religion* (New York, NY: Simon & Schuster, 1930), p. 128.
55 John J. Dunphy, "A Religion for A New Age", *The Humanist*, Vol. 43, No. 1 (JAN-FEB 1983).

> "...the AHA [American Humanist Association] accredits ministers and counselors who can conduct weddings and funerals, develops Humanist literature, proselytizes (only those in agreement with the doctrines are eligible to join) and raises money as **a tax-exempt 'religious' organization**...
>
> Among religions in this country which do not teach what would generally be considered a belief in the existence of God are Buddhism, Taoism, Ethical Culture, **Secular Humanism** and others."

Even secular humanists themselves claim they are a religion. Paul Kurtz, a leading Humanist spokesman who drafted the *Humanist Manifesto II (1973)* **admitted:**

> "There are no Humanist membership organizations that are non-religious in legal status."[56]

Right or wrong, good or bad...can we at least stop pretending that compulsory government schools are religiously neutral and acknowledge that *the *conversion* of students is its *sacred purpose?**

When the consequences of this form of schooling is followed to its natural conclusion...consider the letter that Adolf Hitler wrote to Hermann Rauschning (prior to World War II) regarding the relationship between the individual and the government.

> "Of what importance is all that, if I range men firmly within a discipline they cannot escape? Let them own land or factories as much as they please.

---

56 Robert K. Skolrood, "Evangelism in the Classroom-Humanist Style", Kappa Delta Pi Record (Winter 1988), pp. 46-48.

> "The decisive factor is that **the State**, through the Party, **is supreme over them regardless of whether they are owners or workers**. All that is unessential; **our socialism goes far deeper**. It establishes a **relationship of the individual to the State, the national community**. Why need we trouble to socialize banks and factories? **We socialize human beings**."[57]

In theologian Dietrich Bonhoeffer's brilliant analysis of Nazism, he observed that the *best-schooled nation in the world*—Germany—fell completely under the sway of Hitler's influence. Moreover, Bonhoeffer noted that Nazism could *only be understood* as the psychological product of "good" schooling.

The point here is NOT to employ clichéd comparisons to Nazis in order to demonize America's "Founding Fathers" of compulsory government schooling.

HOWEVER, it *is* important to note both the *mechanisms* and the *results* of the Nazi's educational program…a program that shares several uncomfortable similarities with the compulsory school system advocated by Dewey et. al.

But not everyone drank the Dewey-flavored Kool Aid®.

While the "Founding Fathers" were busy transforming government schooling, there were those who took notice and sounded the alarm.

One of those was New York City Mayor John Hylan who warned in 1922 that:

> "…the **real menace of our republic is this invisible government** which like a giant octopus sprawls its slimy length over city, State and nation.

---

[57] Hermann Rauschning, *The Voice of Destruction* (New York, NY: G. P. Putnam's Son, 1940), pp. 191-193.

"Like the octopus of real life, it operates under cover of self-created screen. It seizes in its long and powerful tentacles our executive officers, **our legislative bodies, our schools, our courts, our newspapers and every agency** created for the public protection."[58]

Tragically, the warnings of Mayor Hylan went largely unheeded until 1952, when Senator William E. Jenner [R-IN] entered the following into the Congressional Record:

"This war against our Constitution...is being fought here... in our schools... colleges... churches... women's clubs. It is being fought with our money, channeled through the State Department. It is being fought 24 hours a day... while we remain asleep...The UN is at work... every day and night, **changing the teachers, changing the teaching materials, changing the very words and tones—changing all the essential ideas which we imagine our schools are teaching to our young folks.**"[59]

And one final thought...consider the influence of Dewey et. al. upon the largest professional organization and labor union in the United States...the 3.2-million-member National Education Association (NEA). The following is a brief overview, *in their own words*, of their agenda for compulsory government schooling.

In 1857, 43 educators met in Philadelphia, PA and founded the National Teachers Association. By 1870, the National Teachers Association had merged with the National Association of School Superintendents and the American Normal School Association to form the National Education Association (NEA).

---

58 Cited in Dennis L. Cuddy, Ph.D., *Chronology of Education With Quotable Quotes* (Highland City, FL: Pro Family Forum, Inc., 1993), pp. 15, 24.
59 Sally D. Reed, *NEA: Propaganda Front of the Radical Left* (Alexandria, VA: National Council for Better Education, 1984).

Membership was later expanded to include "any person in any way connected with the world of education."[60]

Adopted at the 2006 NEA Representative Assembly, the *National Education Association Handbook* (p. 7) described the organization's mission:

> "...to advocate for professionals and to unite our members and the nation to fulfill the promise of public education to prepare every student to succeed in a diverse and interdependent world."[61]

So far, so good. Who can object to preparing students to succeed?

However, the history of the NEA has consistently demonstrated otherwise. In their version of scholastic utopia, (1) parents should be *prevented* from educating their own children, (2) parental authority should be *transferred* to NEA-approved educators, and (3) children should be *conditioned to follow* the edutocracy's agenda.

Echoing Woodrow Wilson's earlier sentiments, Stanford research psychologist and former NEA analyst Gerald W. Bracey, Ph.D., acknowledged:

> "I think we absolutely have to realize that if we were to educate everyone, the country would fall apart... **We absolutely positively have to have a group of undereducated, unskilled people to do all these dirty jobs** that 'the comfortable classes', as John Kenneth Galbraith calls them, will not do.

---

60 Sally D. Reed, *NEA: Propaganda Front of the Radical Left* (Alexandria, VA: National Council for Better Education, 1984).
61 http://www.nea.org/home/19583.htm.

"...until everyone owns a humanoid robot, as well as a car and a color television, some person will have to do the 'dirty jobs.' Until then, however, loath as we are to admit it, **we must continue to produce an uneducated social class...**"[62]

In 1935, NEA Executive Secretary Willard Givens, reported to the 72nd annual NEA meeting:

"...many drastic changes must be made... A dying 'laissez-faire' must be completely destroyed and all of us, including the 'owners', must be **subjected to a large degree of social control...** "The major function of the school is the **social orientation of the individual**. It must seek to give him understanding of the **transition to a new social order**."[63]

In 1947, the NEA's Association for Supervision and Curriculum Development affirmed:

"Far too many people in America, both in and out of education, look upon the elementary school as a place to learn reading, writing and arithmetic."[64]

In 1948, the NEA's "Education for International Understanding in American Schools" report declared:

"Education for international understanding involves the use of education as a force for **conditioning the will of the people**."[65]

---

[62] Gerald W. Bracey, "What If Education Broke Out All Over?", *Education Week* (28 March 1994). Cf. John Kenneth Galbraith, *The Culture of Contentment* (Boston, MA: Houghton Mifflin, 1992).
[63] Samuel L. Blumenfeld, *NEA: Trojan Horse in American Education*, "Introduction" (Phoenix, AZ: The Paradigm Company, 1985).
[64] Association for Supervision and Curriculum Development, National Education Association Yearbook (1947).
[65] National Education Association, "Education for International Understanding in American Schools" (1948), p. 33.

William Paul Haubner of the NEA's Teacher-Rights Division, openly asserted that *parents were an obstacle to education*:

> "The schools **cannot allow parents to influence** the kind of values-education their children receive in school; that is what is wrong with those who say there is a universal system of values. **Our goals are incompatible with theirs.** We must **change their values.**"[66]

In 1962, an editorial published in *The Chicago Sun-Times* confirmed this disturbing trend:

> "...**real control over the nation's children is being shifted rapidly to the NEA.** That organization has about completed the job of cartelizing public schools' education under...an organization known as the National Council for Accreditation of Teachers Education, an agency whose governing council is tightly NEA controlled...
>
> "The manner in which the NEA is usurping parental prerogatives...is...very simple: control the education and hiring of teachers."[67]

In 1969, the NEA's "Education for the '70s" report predicted:

> "**Schools will become clinics** whose purpose is to provide individualized, psycho-social treatment for the student, and **teachers must become psycho-social therapists.**"[68]

---

66 http://www.americanthinker.com/2013/02/schools_jump_the_shark.html
67 Dennis L. Cuddy, Ph.D., *Chronology of Education With Quotable Quotes* (Highland City, FL: Pro Family Forum, Inc., 1993), p. 35.
68 National Education Association, "Education for the '70s", *Today's Education* (January 1969).

In 1970, the NEA's Association for Supervision and Curriculum Development published, "To Nurture Humaneness: Commitment for the '70's," in which John Loughary, Professor of Education at the University of Oregon, outlined their objectives:

> "Many daily decisions and value judgments now made by the individual will soon be made for him... **How to plan for one's children's education will be partially taken out of his [the parents] hands.**"[69]

Later that year, NEA President George Fischer informed the union's annual assembly:

> "...a good deal of work has been done to begin to bring about uniform certification controlled by the unified profession in each state... With these new laws, **we will finally realize our 113-year-old dream of controlling who enters, who stays and leaves the profession.**

> "[...] we can also **control the teacher training institutions.**"[70]

In 1976, Harold Shane, Project Director for the NEA Bicentennial Committee published a report that employed many of the same buzzwords characterizing outcome-based education today:

> "Rather than adding my voice to those who urge us to go 'back to the basics', I would argue that **we need to move ahead to new basics...** Certainly, cross-cultural understanding and empathy have become fundamental skills of human relations and intercultural rapport...

---

[69] NEA, "To Nurture Humaneness: Commitment for the '70's" (Washington, DC: Association for Supervision and Curriculum Development, 1970), pp. 50-51, 79, 106-107, 181.
[70] Peter Brimelow & Leslie Spencer, "The National Extortion Association", *Forbes* (7 June 1993), p. 74.

"the arts of compromise and reconciliation, of **consensus building**, and of planning for **interdependence**, a command of these talents becomes 'basics'...

"As young people mature, we must help them develop... a service ethic which is geared toward the real world... **the global servant concept in which we will educate our young for planetary service and eventually for some form of world citizenship.**"[71]

With all due respect Mr. Shane (assuming you have children), I seriously doubt that parents send their kids to public school for the same reasons you think they do.

Since John Dewey (remember him?) was an honorary life-time president of the National Education Association, there are two equally troubling points to absorb here:[72]

1. The NEA was founded on the belief that, "Parental rights and religious freedom would be swallowed up by the surpassing rights and rules of the greater community—the controlled collective."

2. The NEA intends "...to create the kinds of schools and curricula which would produce, if not perfect men, at least the kinds of men and women the educators considered desirable."

Apparently, controlling and conditioning children is how the NEA defines "prepar[ing] every student to succeed." At least they are honest about their agenda...*scary and twisted*...but honest.

---

71 Harold Shane, "America's Next 25 Years: Some Implications for Education," *Phi Delta Kappan* (September 1976). Cf. Dennis L. Cuddy, Ph.D., *Chronology of Education With Quotable Quotes* (Highland City, FL: Pro Family Forum, Inc., 1993), p. 59.
72 Samuel L. Blumenfeld, *NEA: Trojan Horse in American Education* (Phoenix, AZ: The Paradigm Company, 1985), p. 31.

Perhaps American intellectual and essayist **H. L. Mencken (1880-1956)** described compulsory government schooling best:

> "The aim of public education is not to spread enlightenment at all, it is simply to **reduce as many individuals as possible to the same safe level**, to breed and **train a standardized citizenry**, to put down dissent and originality. **That is its aim in the United States**, whatever the pretensions of politicians, pedagogues and other such mountebanks [deceivers], and that is its aim everywhere else."[73]

SIDENOTE: Anthony Esolen's, *Ten Ways To Destroy the Imagination of Your Child (2010),* does a masterful job of describing precisely how to accomplish what the title of his book suggests.

The similarities between his tongue-in-cheek prescriptions and the actual products of our public school system (namely standardized, predictable mediocrity)...are both insightful and eerily accurate.

---

[73] H. L. Mencken, *The American Mercury* (April 1924).

PART II

How are we doing?

PART II: How are we doing?

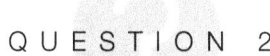

QUESTION 2

How did this book come about?

For fourteen years, I loved every minute of teaching high school history, economics, government, and speech/debate, and have spoken at numerous home-school conferences and educational seminars.

These wonderful experiences blessed me with the unique opportunity to field countless questions from a wide variety of audiences concerning educational issues. In fact, this book is almost entirely based upon the most frequently asked questions that I have received since 2002.

Although Americans generally agree that our public school system has problems requiring immediate attention…the real debate concerns the prescription.

Unfortunately, compulsory government schools at every level are performing worse than you think…*far worse*.

Tragically, as you have already learned from **PART I: How did we get here?**…this is *entirely by design*.

QUESTION 3

How well have compulsory government schools addressed the acquisition of knowledge?

According to the evidence…not well.

James Madison (1751-1836) once remarked that, "Knowledge will forever govern ignorance; and a people who mean to be their own governors must arm themselves with the power which knowledge gives."[74]

"A Nation At Risk"—the landmark report commissioned by President Ronald Reagan's National Commission on Excellence in Education and published in April of 1983—is widely considered the most important research document in modern American educational history. The following excerpt is especially alarming:

> "If an unfriendly foreign power had attempted to impose on America the **mediocre educational performance** that exists today, we might well have viewed it as **an act of war**. As it stands, **we have allowed this to happen to ourselves**. We have even **squandered the gains in student achievement** made in the wake of the Sputnik challenge.

---

74 Philip B. Kurland & Ralph Lerner, eds., *The Founders Constitution*, "Epilogue: Securing the Republic," (Chicago, IL: Chicago University Press, 2000), Chapter 18, Document 35. Letter from James Madison to W. T. Barry, 4 August 1822.

"Moreover, we have **dismantled essential support systems**, which helped make those gains possible. We have, in effect, been committing an act of **unthinking, unilateral educational disarmament.**"[75]

And this was the state of public-school education in 1983...consider where it's at now.

---

75 "A Nation at Risk: The Imperative For Educational Reform" (April 1983). http://www2.ed.gov/pubs/NatAtRisk/risk.html.

QUESTION 4

The implications of "A Nation At Risk" are truly horrifying, but certainly government schooling in America has improved since 1983. Right?

I guess it depends on your definition of "improved."

Although the real-world value of standardized test scores is *dubious at best*, it remains the compulsory government school system's preferred metric of assessment for both achievement and progress. Consider the following examples.

According to the National Center for Education Statistics (NCES):[76]

> "...the National Assessment of Educational Progress (NAEP) is **the only nationally representative and continuing assessment of what America's students know and can do in various subject areas**. Assessments are conducted periodically in mathematics, reading, science, writing, the arts, civics, economics, geography, and U.S. history.
>
> "Since NAEP assessments are administered uniformly using the same sets of test booklets across the nation, NAEP results serve as a common metric for all states and selected urban districts. The assessment stays essentially the same from year to year, with only carefully documented changes. **This permits NAEP to provide a clear picture of student academic progress over time.**"

---

76 http://nces.ed.gov/nationsreportcard/about/. Accessed 11 March 2012.

Since the U.S. national debt has reached $17 trillion ($118 trillion if you include the unfunded liabilities of Social Security and Medicare, A, B, C, D)[77], one could reasonably suggest that economic intelligence should be a top national priority.

However, judging by the actual results, it doesn't even make the top ten. The economic ignorance displayed by U.S. 12th-graders is absolutely breathtaking.

According to the NAEP Assessment (2006)[78] conducted by the National Center for Educational Statistics (NCES) and administered to U.S. 12th-graders:

- Only 36% could identify the federal government's primary source of income [I'll take "The IRS & Taxes" for $500, Alex].

- Only 33% could explain how an increase in real interest rates impacts consumer borrowing.

- Only 11% could analyze how changes in unemployment rates affect income, spending, and production.

- Overall, only 42% of 12th-graders were "at or above proficient" in Economics.[79]

In the subjects of Mathematics, Reading, U.S. History, Science, Civics, and Economics...American 4th-, 8th-, and 12th-graders are also failing...MISERABLY.[80]

---

77 http://www.ncpa.org/pdfs/A_Bleak_Future.pdf.
78 http://www.creators.com/opinion/jackie-gingrich-cushman/raising-children-and-raising-a-nation.html. Citing Marybeth Hicks, *Don't Let the Kids Drink the Kool-Aid* (Washington, DC: Regnery, 2011).
79 https://www.nationsreportcard.gov/economics_2012/overall.aspx#1-0
80 U.S. Department of Education, Institute of Education Sciences, National Center for Education Statistics, National Assessment of Educational Progress (NAEP), https://www.nationsreportcard.gov/.

The NAEP scores in Mathematics...

- 4th-graders (2015) – ONLY 40% "at or above proficient"
- 8th-graders (2015) – ONLY 33% "at or above proficient"
- 12th-graders (2015) – ONLY 25% "at or above proficient"

The NAEP scores in Reading...

- 4th-graders (2015) – ONLY 36% "at or above proficient"
- 8th-graders (2015) – ONLY 34% "at or above proficient"
- 12th-graders (2015) – ONLY 37% "at or above proficient"

The NAEP scores in U.S. History...

- 4th-graders (2010) – ONLY 22% "at or above proficient"
- 8th-graders (2014) – ONLY 18% "at or above proficient"
- 12th-graders (2010) – ONLY 13% "at or above proficient"

The NAEP scores in Science...

- 4th-graders (2015) – ONLY 38% "at or above proficient"
- 8th-graders (2015) – ONLY 34% "at or above proficient"
- 12th-graders (2015) – ONLY 22% "at or above proficient"

The NAEP scores in Civics...

- 4th-graders (2010) – ONLY 29% "at or above proficient"
- 8th-graders (2014) – ONLY 23% "at or above proficient"
- 12th-graders (2010) – ONLY 28% "at or above proficient"

The NAEP scores in Economics...

- 4th-graders – N/A
- 8th-graders – N/A
- 12th-graders (2012) – ONLY 42% "at or above proficient"

The scores speak for themselves...and remember that the "proficiency" bar has been set embarrassingly low.

Another standardized test, the SAT (formerly the Scholastic Assessment Test or Scholastic Aptitude Test) is:

- ❑ Developed, published, and scored by the College Board.
- ❑ Administered by the Educational Testing Service (ETS).
- ❑ Universally accepted as the "gatekeeper" for college admissions.

According to the College Board website:

> "The SAT and SAT Subject Tests are a suite of tools **designed to assess your academic readiness for college**... [and] **measur[e] the skills required for success in the 21st century.**"[81] [*In 2004, the original assessment format was "re-centered" to achieve greater "academic accessibility"—read dumbed down*].

From 1990-1991 to 2008-2009, the average "Critical Reading" score was 463 out of 800 (57.8% or F+) and the average "Mathematics" score was 514 out of 800 (64.3% or D).[82][83]

It should go without saying that these "less-than-stellar" standardized tests won't be posted on anyone's refrigerator door...

---

81 http://sat.collegeboard.org/about-tests. Accessed 5 September 2012.
82 Initially, the test was named the Scholastic Aptitude Test (SAT). In 1993, the SAT was renamed the SAT Reasoning Test (SAT I). Meanwhile, the former Scholastic Achievement Test was renamed the SAT Subject Tests (SAT II).
83 U.S. Department of Education, National Center for Education Statistics, (2010); *Digest of Education Statistics*, 2009 (NCES 2010-013), Chapter 2. http://nces.ed.gov/fastfacts/display.asp?id=171. Accessed 11 October 2011.

QUESTION 5

Admittedly, our NAEP and SAT scores are terrible, but that is only because our national academic standards are so rigorous. Certainly, we compare more favorably against the rest of the world. Right?

———

Actually, U.S. literacy scores in Mathematics, Reading, and Science are—to put it charitably—DISMAL. Since the NAEP works closely with the following highly regarded international testing organizations, *their combined results are especially compelling evidence of systemic failure*.

❑ The **Program for International Student Assessment (PISA)**, sponsored by the Organization for Economic Cooperation and Development (OECD) was established in 2000 to assesses the *mathematics, reading, and science literacy* of 15-year-olds every three years.

❑ The **Progress in International Reading Literacy Study (PIRLS)**, sponsored by the International Association for the Evaluation of Educational Achievement (IEA) was established in 2001 to assess the *reading literacy* of 4th-graders every five years.

❑ The **Trends in International Mathematics and Science Study (TIMSS)**, sponsored by the International Association for the Evaluation of Educational Achievement (IEA) was established in 1995 to assess the *mathematics and science literacy* of both 4th- and 8th-graders every four years.

The United States is lagging behind in *reading literacy*...

- According to the **Program for International Student Assessment (PISA)** (2000, 2003, 2006)[84] the average score for U.S. 15-year-olds was 495 out of a possible 1000, *or 49.5%, an F-*.

- According to the **Progress in International Reading Literacy Study (PIRLS)** (2001, 2006)[85] [86] the average score for U.S. 4th graders was 541 out of a possible 1000, *or 54.1%, an F*.

The United States is lagging behind in *mathematics literacy*...

- According to the **Program for International Student Assessment (PISA)** (2003, 2006)[87] [88] the average score for U.S. 15-year-olds was 479 out of a possible 1000, *or 47.9%, an F-*.

---

84 Organization for Economic Cooperation and Development (OECD), Program for International Student Assessment (PISA), 2000, 2003, 2006.
85 International Association for the Evaluation of Educational Achievement, Progress in International Reading Literacy (PIRLS), 2001 and 2006.
86 J. R. Campbell, D. L. Kelly, I. V. S. Mullis, M. O. Martin & M. Sainsbury, "Framework and Specifications for PIRLS Assessment 2001," 2nd ed. (Chestnut Hill, MA: TIMSS and PIRLS International Study Center, Lynch School of Education, Boston College, 2001).
87 S. Baldi, Y. Jin, M. Skemer, P. J. Green & D. Herget, "Highlights From PISA 2006: Performance of U.S. 15-Year-Old Students in Science and Mathematics Literacy in an International Context," (NCES 2008–016), National Center for Education Statistics, Institute of Education Sciences (Washington, DC: U.S. Department of Education, 2007).
88 M. Lemke, A. Sen, E. Pahlke, L. Partelow, D. Miller, T. Williams, D. Kastberg & L. Jocelyn, "International Outcomes of Learning in Mathematics Literacy and Problem Solving: PISA 2003 Results From the U.S. Perspective," (NCES 2005-003R), National Center for Education Statistics, (Washington, DC: U.S. Department of Education, 2004).

❑ According to the **Trends in International Mathematics and Science Study (TIMSS)** (2003, 2007)[89][90] the average score for U.S. 4th-graders was 524 out of a possible 1000, *or 52.4%, an F* AND for U.S. 8th-graders it was 506 out of a possible 1000, *or 50.6%, an F.*

Finally, in keeping with the results of the other tests, the United States is also lagging behind in *science literacy*…

❑ According to the **Trends in International Mathematics and Science Study (TIMSS)** (2003, 2007)[91] the average score for U.S. 4th-graders was 538 out of a possible 1000, *or 53.8%, an F* AND for U.S. 8th-graders it was 524 out of a possible 1000, *or 52.4%, an F.*

❑ According to the **Program for International Student Assessment (PISA)** (2000, 2003, 2006)[92][93] the average score for U.S. 15-year-olds was 493 out of a possible 1000, *or 49.3%, an F-.*

---

89 I. V. S. Mullis, M. O. Martin, P. Foy, J. F. Olson, C. Preuschoff, E. Erberber, A. Arora, J. Galia, "TIMSS 2007 International Mathematics Report: Findings from IEA's Trends in International Mathematics and Science Study at the Fourth and Eighth Grades" (Chestnut Hill, MA: TIMSS & PIRLS International Study Center, Boston College, 2008).
http://timss.bc.edu/TIMSS2007/PDF/T07_M_IR_Chapter1.pdf.
90 International Association for the Evaluation of Educational Achievement (IEA), Trends in International Mathematics and Science Study (TIMSS), 2003.
http://nces.ed.gov/timss/timss03tables.asp?Quest=1&Figure=1.
91 M. O. Martin, I. V. S. Mullis, P. Foy, J. F. Olson, E. Erberber, C. Preuschoff & J. Galia, "TIMSS 2007 International Science Report: Findings from IEA's Trends in International Mathematics and Science Study at the Fourth and Eighth Grades" (Chestnut Hill, MA: TIMSS & PIRLS International Study Center, Boston College, 2008).
http://timss.bc.edu/TIMSS2007/PDF/T07_S_IR_Chapter1.pdf.
92 Organization for Economic Cooperation and Development (OECD), Program for International Student Assessment (PISA), 2000, 2003, 2006.
93 S. Baldi, Y. Jin, M. Skemer, P. J. Green & D. Herget, "Highlights From PISA 2006: Performance of U.S. 15-Year-Old Students in Science and Mathematics Literacy in an International Context," (NCES 2008–016), National Center for Education Statistics, Institute of Education Sciences (Washington, DC: U.S. Department of Education, 2007).

BOTTOM LINE: There are several countries rapidly advancing in reading, mathematics, and science literacy while the United States is *often barely at—or only slightly above—*the international averages in those subjects.

QUESTION 6

Even though our NAEP, SAT, PISA, PIRLS, and TIMSS scores are consistently below mediocre, at least our literacy rates are among the highest in the world. Right?

The **CIA World Factbook** defines "literacy" as the percent of a country's population, age 15 and older, who can read and write.[94] Though a few of the world literacy rates listed below represent estimates dating back to 1999 (or even earlier) it remains a tragic fact that several countries have HIGHER literacy rates *than even the highest-scoring U.S. states*.

In fact, the following countries all have *higher* literacy rates than our highest scoring states (U.S. states are recorded in ALL CAPS and **bolded**)…

Andorra, Finland, Georgia [Eurasia], Greenland, Liechtenstein, Luxembourg, Norway, Vatican City, Cuba, Estonia, Poland, Barbados, Latvia, Samoa, Slovenia, Belarus, Lithuania, Slovakia, Kazakhstan, Tajikistan, Armenia, Hungary, Russia, Ukraine, Uzbekistan, Moldova, Australia, Belgium, Canada, Czech Republic, Denmark, France, Germany, Great Britain, Northern Ireland, Iceland, Ireland, Japan, North Korea, Monaco, Netherlands, New Zealand, Saint Pierre & Miquelon, Sweden, Switzerland, Tonga, Azerbaijan, Guyana, Turkmenistan, Albania, Kyrgyzstan, Trinidad & Tobago, Italy, Bulgaria, Croatia, Austria, Bermuda, Cayman Islands, French Polynesia, Turks & Caicos Islands, Uruguay, South Korea, Spain, British Virgin Islands,

---

94 https://www.cia.gov/library/publications/the-world-factbook/fields/2103.html#xx. Accessed 3 October 2011.

Mongolia, Saint Kitts & Nevis, Cyprus, Aruba, Romania, Argentina, Israel, American Samoa, Montserrat, Northern Mariana Islands, Saint Helena, Bosnia & Herzegovina, Netherlands Antilles, Serbia, Maldives, New Caledonia, Macedonia, Taiwan-China, Greece, Grenada, Saint Vincent & the Grenadines, San Marino, Chile, Bahamas, Anguilla, Cook Islands, Niue, Costa Rica, Puerto Rico, Dominica, Paraguay, **MINNESOTA, NEW HAMPSHIRE, NORTH DAKOTA**, Fiji Islands, Marshall Islands, Hong Kong, Kuwait, Portugal, Venezuela, **IOWA, MAINE, MISSOURI, NEBRASKA, SOUTH DAKOTA, VERMONT, WISCONSIN**, Peru, Malta, Brunei, Philippines, Thailand, Singapore, Palestinian Territories, Palau, **INDIANA, KANSAS, MICHIGAN, RHODE ISLAND**, Kosovo, Panama, Seychelles, Macau, Ecuador, Mexico, **CONNECTICUT, MONTANA, OHIO, UTAH, WYOMING**, China, Sri Lanka, Zimbabwe, Colombia, Indonesia, Vietnam, Saint Lucia, **COLORADO, MASSACHUSETTS, OREGON, WASHINGTON**, Jordan, Myanmar, Suriname, Federated States of Micronesia, Qatar, **DELAWARE, IDAHO, MARYLAND**, Malaysia, Brazil, **KENTUCKY, OKLAHOMA, VIRGINIA**, Jamaica, Lebanon, Turkey, Dominican Republic, Equatorial Guinea, **ARIZONA, ILLINOIS, PENNSYLVANIA, TENNESSEE, WEST VIRGINIA**, Bolivia, Bahrain, South Africa, **ARKANSAS, NORTH CAROLINA**, Antigua & Barbuda, Kenya, Namibia, **ALABAMA, SOUTH CAROLINA**, Republic of Congo, **GEORGIA, NEW JERSEY**, Libya, Swaziland, Oman, Botswana, **ALASKA, DISTRICT OF COLUMBIA, TEXAS**, Zambia, El Salvador, Gibraltar, Honduras, FLORIDA, Syria, Saudi Arabia, **NEW YORK** (78%), United Arab Emirates, Iran, and **CALIFORNIA** (77%).

BOTTOM LINE: For the self-appointed education "experts" who mindlessly intone the mythological virtues of compulsory government schooling, it is clear they will have to rely on evidence other than national/international standardized test scores and literacy rates.

QUESTION 7

Even though our NAEP, SAT, PISA, PIRLS, TIMSS scores, and literacy rates are perilously substandard, the only reason that U.S. students are lagging so far behind their international peers is because the federal government doesn't spend enough money on the problem. Right?

Actually, the amount of money spent on public education by the federal government can be probably best described as a "prohibitively expensive failure that drains our national economy and wastes the precious time of our students."

According to the U.S. Department of Education, between 1960-61 and 2006-07, federal spending per student jumped from $3,068 (2014 USD) to $11,327 (2014 USD).[95]

---

95 U.S. Department of Education, National Center for Education Statistics, Digest of Education Statistics: 2010, NCES 2010-013 (2009), Tables 180, 182 and Chapter 2. NOTE: Beginning in 1980-1981, state administration expenditures were excluded from "current" expenditures. These "current" expenditures include instruction, student support services, food services and enterprise operations. Beginning in 1988-1989, extensive changes were made in the data collection procedures.

This spending represents *an increase of 269%*...to achieve an average national graduation rate of *74 percent.* [96] [97]

---

96 Economist Stephen J. Dubner of *Freakonomics* fame asserts that the national graduation rates are even lower than reported. Citing a new working paper written by James Heckman and Paul LaFontaine entitled "The American High School Graduation Rate: Trends and Levels," Dubner notes that the authors employ multiple data sources and a unified methodology to estimate trends and levels of the U.S. high school graduation rate. Correcting for important biases that plague previous calculations, they establish that the true high school graduation rate is substantially lower than the official rate issued by the National Center for Education Statistics and has been declining over the past 40 years.
97 http://www.westegg.com/inflation/.

QUESTION 8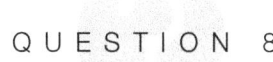

Since the federal government spends so lavishly on public schooling, state governments must be to blame for not contributing enough money. Right?

I guess that depends on what you consider "enough."

In 2008-2009, the 50 states (including Washington, DC) produced the following results:

- The national average spending per student was $11,557 (2014 USD).[98]
- The national average graduation rate was 75.5%.[99]
- The national average dropout rate was 4.1%.[100]
- The national average literacy rate was 88%.[101]
- The national average reading proficiency rate was 41.8%.[102]
- The national average math proficiency rate was 32.2%.[103]

As a parent and/or taxpayer, would you describe the results produced by this extravagant spending at both the federal and state levels as "money well spent?"

---

98 http://www2.census.gov/govs/school/09f33pub.pdf. Accessed 13 September 2011.
99 http://nces.ed.gov/pubs2011/2011312.pdf. Accessed 13 September 2011.
100 http://nces.ed.gov/pubs2011/2011312.pdf. Accessed 13 September 2011.
101 https://www.cia.gov/library/publications/the-world-factbook/fields/2103.html#xx. Accessed 3 October 2011.
102 http://www.hks.harvard.edu/pepg/PDF/Papers/PEPG11-03_GloballyChallenged.pdf. Accessed 13 September 2011.
103 http://www.hks.harvard.edu/pepg/PDF/Papers/PEPG11-03_GloballyChallenged.pdf. Accessed 13 September 2011.

QUESTION 9

But since not all states spend the same amount of money on education, the five states spending the most money must be producing the best results. Right?

You would think so...but...um...NO.

❑ In 2008-2009, the state of *Vermont spent $16,704 (2014 USD) per student* to achieve a high school graduation rate of 89.6% and a literacy rate of 93%. With a high school dropout rate of 1.1%, *only* 42.1% of their students were proficient in reading, while a *mere* 41.4% were proficient in mathematics.

❑ In 2008-2009, the state of *Alaska spent $17,118 (2014 USD) per student* to achieve a high school graduation rate of 72.6% and a literacy rate of 81%. With a high school dropout rate of 7.0%, *only* 43.7% of their students were proficient in reading, while a *mere* 32.2% were proficient in mathematics.

❑ In 2008-2009, the state of *New Jersey spent $17,910 (2014 USD)* per student to achieve a high school graduation rate of 85.3% and a literacy rate of 83%. With a high school dropout rate of 1.6%, *only* 51.4% of their students were proficient in reading, while a *mere* 40.4% were proficient in mathematics.

❑ In 2008-2009, the *District of Columbia spent $18,062 (2014 USD) per student* to achieve a high school graduation rate of 62.4% and a literacy rate of 81%. With a high school dropout rate of 7.0%, *only* 12.1% of their students were proficient in reading, while a *mere* 8.0% were proficient in mathematics.

❑ In 2008-2009, the state of *New York spent $19,952 (2014 USD) per student* to achieve a high school graduation rate of 73.5% and a literacy rate of 78%. With a high school dropout rate of 4.2%, *only* 39.1% of their students were proficient in reading, while a *mere* 30.2% were proficient in mathematics.

When you add the average *federal spending per student of $11,327 (2014 USD)* to the average *state spending per student of $11,557 (2014 USD)*…the federal government and the 50 states (including Washington, DC) *collectively spend $22,884 (2014 USD) per student, per year* to "achieve":[104][105][106]

❑ A national high school graduation rate of 75.5%.
❑ A national literacy rate of 88%.
❑ A national dropout rate of 4.1%.
❑ A national reading proficiency of *only* 41.8%.
❑ A national mathematics proficiency of *just* 32.2%.

As a tax-paying parent…*do you think that you know better than educrats* how to *spend $22,884 per year, per child* to give your son(s) and/or daughter(s) a great education?

---

[104] Digest of Education Statistics 2009, National Center for Education Statistics, Table 59. http://www.capenet.org/facts.html
[105] Stephen J. Dubner, "Is the U.S. High School Graduation Rate Worse Than We Thought?" *New York Times* (27 December 2007).
[106] U.S. Department of Education, National Center for Education Statistics, Digest of Education Statistics: 2007, Table 174. http://nces.ed.gov/programs/digest/d07/tables/dt07_a174.asp (19 August 2008).

By the way, if your child attended school from K-12, that figure would total *$297,492 (2014 USD)* by the time they graduated. So, just ask yourself this one simple question:

Would your child be graduating from high school with $297,492 worth of education?

QUESTION 10

If the federal and state governments are spending so much money to produce such abysmal results, then the fault must lie with local school districts who are under-spending on education. Right?

Um...under-spending?

Consider the Los Angeles Unified School District (LAUSD), the second-largest school district in America...and decide for yourself.

Since 2001, the LAUSD has built and/or renovated:[107]

❏ The *$626 million (2014 USD) Robert F. Kennedy High School*—the most expensive government-run K-12 school in this nation's history—that opened in 2010 and serves 4,200 students.

❏ The *$418 million (2014 USD) Edward R. Roybal Learning Center* (formerly Belmont Learning Center) that opened in 2008 and serves 2,500 students.

❏ The *$256 million (2014 USD) Visual and Performing Arts High School* that opened in 2009 and serves 1,700 students.

---

107 Staff writers, "LAUSD builds monuments to its questionable spending", *Daily Breeze* (15 July 2010).

- The *$206 million (2014 USD)*, 29-story, 928,000-square-foot tower at 333 S. Beaudry Avenue that opened in 2001 and is occupied by over 3,400 district employees.[108]

BOTTOM LINE: The LAUSD spent an unbelievable *$1.3 billion (2014 USD) on just three schools* **to "educate"** *8,400 students* at the astronomical cost of *$154,761.90 per student.*[109] [110] [111] [112]

If you think that spending $1.3 billion is "just what things cost these days", compare the LAUSD's construction costs to these multi-million-dollar Los Angeles facilities built in recent years:

- The *$835 million (2014 USD) Hollywood & Highland complex* opened in 2001.

- The *$527 million (2014 USD) Staples Center* **(seats 19,079)** opened in 1999.

- The *$439 million (2014 USD) Americana at Brand* **opened in 2008.**

- The *$351 million (2014 USD) Walt Disney Concert Hall* **(seats 2,265)** opened in 2003.

- The *$248 million (2014 USD) Cathedral of Our Lady of the Angels* **(seats 4,100) opened in 2002.**

---

108 Justino Aguila & Beth Barrett, "Beaudry building in downtown L.A. a pricey place for LAUSD personnel", *Daily News* (28 September 2008).
109 Staff writers, "LAUSD builds monuments to its questionable spending", *Daily Breeze* (15 July 2010).
110 Justino Aguila & Beth Barrett, "Beaudry building in downtown L.A. a pricey place for LAUSD personnel", *Daily News* (28 September 2008).
111 Lance T. Izumi, JD, "That sucking sound is LAUSD doing business as usual", *Daily News* (1 September 2010).
112 http://www.westegg.com/inflation/.

- The *$217 million (2014 USD) back lot at Universal Studios* opened in 2010.

- The *$192 million (2014 USD) Home Depot Center* (seats 27,000) opened in 2003.

FYI: The *$548 million (2014 USD) Bird's Nest stadium* (seats 91,000) opened in 2008 for the Olympic Games in Beijing, China. [*Yes, I know that labor costs are lower in China, but I'm just sayin'*].[113]

While we're on the subject of things the LAUSD wastes money on, consider the following:[114] [115] [116]

- During 2009-2010, with an operating budget of "only" $7.3 billion, the LAUSD served 693,680 students, managed 837 schools, and employed 45,473 teachers, 38,494 "other staff", and 849 consultants.

- Of those 84,816 LAUSD employees, approximately 4,000 administrators, managers, and other non-school-based personnel—not including clerks and office workers—earned an *annual salary of nearly $95,000*.

- Of those 3,478 LAUSD employees who earned an *annual salary of $100,000* or more, approximately 2,400 of that number were administrators.

- The LAUSD's 45,473 teachers earned an average *annual salary of $63,000*, while the average *annual household income* in Los Angeles County was *less than $73,000*.

---

113 http://abcnews.go.com/Business/wireStory?id=11456538.
114 http://www.dailynews.com/news/ci_10579906.
115 http://www.dailynews.com/news/ci_10585677.
116 Lance T. Izumi, J.D., "That sucking sound is LAUSD doing business as usual", *Daily News* (1 September 2010).

- ❏ From 2001 to 2006, during Roy Romer's tenure as superintendent, the LAUSD bureaucracy *exploded by 18%...even as student enrollment DECLINED by 6% and 500 teaching positions were eliminated.*

- ❏ Between 2001 and 2007, district enrollment *fell 6%* while the number of LAUSD administrators *rose by nearly 20%.*

- ❏ In 2009, the district's inspector general reported that the LAUSD paid *$220 million (2014 USD) to 1,700 employees no longer on the job.*

- ❏ In 2009, the LAUSD paid *$30 million for 900 positions* not funded in its budget.

Sort of makes you wonder how many taxpayer dollars are being wasted in the *other* 13,584 public school districts across the United States?

QUESTION 11

Even if the LAUSD squandered most of their $7.3 billion budget, at least the money made a positive difference for their students. Right?

If you think that low graduation rates, high dropout rates, low literacy rates, and low reading and mathematics proficiency rates are "making a difference"...then yes, the money was well spent.

❏ According to a 2006 study published by *Education Week*, the LAUSD's graduation rate ranked among the worst in the nation at 44% while their self-reported dropout rate stood at 33%.[117]

❏ In 2008, the district claimed it spent $10,000 per pupil (NOTE: figure excludes bond-financed building costs or interest costs on those bonds). However, according to Adam Schaeffer, a researcher at the Washington, DC-based Cato Institute and the author of a study that analyzed district spending, when construction-related and other non-counted costs were included, *the district's real per-pupil funding figure was $29,790.*[118]

❏ From 2008 to 2010, auditors reported that *unnecessary textbook purchases and other boondoggles cost the district nearly $10 million.* For instance, $500,000 worth of unused

---

117 Harrison Sheppard, "LAUSD's graduation rate: 44%", *Daily News* (21 June 2006). Cf. http://www.csun.edu/pubrels/clips/June07/06-13-07G.pdf
118 http://www.cato.org/pubs/pas/pa662.pdf. Accessed 13 October 2011.

textbooks sat in a district warehouse for several years. Even more frightening… *the audit only examined 21 of 100 high schools in just that district.*[119]

NOTE: Since district high schools use such outdated and substandard textbook inventory systems…and elementary schools have no system at all…one can only imagine the massive losses spread across America's 13,584 public school districts.

BOTTOM LINE: Hand-wringing "educrats" notwithstanding, money is obviously not the cure for our precipitous descent into the academic abyss.

Hysterical public-school apologists, self-appointed education "experts", and teachers' unions reflexively lament inadequate funding as the cause of all our educational woes.

However, the epic failure of these educrats becomes absolutely sickening when one considers the billions of taxpayer dollars (e.g., federal, state, and local) they have already "invested" to produce such unconscionably poor results.

---

119 http://www.cato.org/pubs/pas/pa662.pdf. Accessed 13 October 2011.

QUESTION 12

If—according to their own metrics—compulsory government schooling is an abject failure and a colossal waste of money, then what exactly are educrats doing to improve it?

Sam Blumenfeld wrote a brilliant article entitled, "Have Government Schools Become a Criminal Enterprise?" for *The New American* (23 June 2010) that described the crimes...er... "action plans" of these educrats in uncomfortable detail.

Proving that principles are nearly non-existent in politics, President George W. Bush [R-TX] and Senator Ted Kennedy [D-MA] were *widely praised* for re-authorizing the **Elementary and Secondary Education Act of 1965**...which simply rebranded mediocrity as the **No Child Left Behind Act (2001)**.

Remember that Congress extorted... er... "funded" this legislation with *taxpayer dollars*.

As Blumenfeld insightfully observes:

> "Extortion is also part of the routine criminality **practiced by our educators**. For example, since 1965, the federal government has been funding Title One of the ESEA which provides compensatory education for socially and economically deprived children in the inner cities. So far, in 38 years, **over $125 billion** has been spent on the program with **no improvement** in the academic skills of these students. In other words, **over $125 billion of taxpayers' money** has been used in ways that have **not served the purposes of compensatory education.** Isn't this

misuse of money called extortion, and isn't extortion considered a crime?"

Perhaps we should pause here to define the word "crime"? In 1850, Noah Webster described "crime" as:

> "An act which violates a law, divine or human; an act which violates a rule of moral duty; an offense against the laws of right, prescribed by God or man, or against any rule of duty implied in these laws. A crime may consist in omission or neglect, as well as in commission, or positive transgression."[120]

Since America's public schools are awash in moral relativism, isn't it rather hypocritical for educrats to insist that teachers fulfill their "moral duty" to teach students to read, write, and perform arithmetic? Nevertheless, all 50 state constitutions require that all children be educated in these basic subjects.

In addition to these criminal acts, educrats also serve as legalized drug dealers who force millions of students to take mind-altering pharmaceuticals in order to more easily control and indoctrinate... er... "socialize" them with substandard schooling.

In the same article, Blumenfeld also addresses the widely-discredited whole-word method (e.g., Whole Language) that *"deliberately creates reading disabilit[ies] and the condition called dyslexia."*

Children instinctively realize something terrible is being done to them, but *"they don't know how it is being done"* or *"how to articulate what is being done."* Consequently, they become angry and frustrated, and their behavior often reflects an understandable hatred of schooling.

---

[120] *Webster's New World Dictionary* (1988), omits, "an act which violates a rule of moral duty."

Naturally, these angry children are then labeled as *"problem students"*, and present educrats with a *"perfectly plausible reason for drugging the kids."*

Sadly, many parents prefer to *"believe a credible lie…that there is something wrong with Johnny than an incredible truth…that their child is the victim of deliberate educational malpractice."*

It's hardly surprising then, that this form of "educational malpractice" has inspired a typical, knee-jerk educratic solution to lagging scores…increase funding for "Head Start" (the flagship pre-kindergarten program introduced in 1965 that has become an embarrassing $166 billion monument to failure).[121]

❏ Though a few modest improvements in language skills were recorded, the Department of Health and Human Services (HHS) study reported that *by the end of first grade, even the effects of those minor advances have disappeared*.

❏ Only *2 out of 44* separate cognitive tests given to former Head Start students at the end of the first grade showed even *marginally significant effects*.[122]

❏ And *42 out of 44* separate cognitive tests given to former Head Start students at the end of the first grade showed *no statistically significant effect at all*.

---

121 http://www.acf.hhs.gov/programs/opre/hs/impact_study/reports/impact_study/executive_summary_final.pdf.
122 For each of the 44 separate tests, there is a 1 in 10 chance of recording a false positive (a test result that appears to show a positive impact but is actually a random fluke). The authors of the study controlled for the tests to account for any likelihood of false positives and found (1) no "socio-emotional" benefits, (2) no "parenting practice" benefits, and (3) that the two apparently "significant" effects vanished.

BOTTOM LINE: A total of *$166 billion dollars* was wasted to finance the myth that educrats were "doing something" to "improve" government schooling.

CHAPTER 13

Since the money that compulsory government schools spend is going somewhere, educrats must be spending it to educate, train, and hire the best teachers. Right?

NOTE: It should go without saying here that *most teachers are noble and dedicated individuals who deeply desire to make a positive difference in the lives of their students*...but every profession has its failures.

Moreover, tenure grants incompetent teachers a level of job security unmatched by any other profession... unless you work for the federal government.

In 2008, the College Board issued a press release[123] that revealed (1) high school graduates who intend to major in education *scored in the bottom third of the SAT* compared to 36 other intended majors and (2) nationally, these potential education majors finished *25th in reading, 27th in math, and a combined 57 points below the national SAT average in both*.

Since our compulsory government school system places such a premium on standardized test scores, how can educrats claim that the "best and brightest" collegians are aspiring teachers?

Consider the following:

---

123 Ron Matus, "SAT scores of teacher wannabes", *Tampa Bay Times* (2 September 2008). http://press.collegeboard.org/releases/2008/sat174-scores-stable-record-numbers-take-test. Accessed 17 September 2012.

- ❑ An Associate Arts degree (AA) is traditionally a two-year program of study particular to a specific field and typically requires the completion of 64 credits in prescribed course work.

- ❑ A Bachelor of Arts degree (BA) is traditionally a four-year program of study particular to a specific field and typically requires the completion of 120 credits in prescribed course work with a minimum of 45 credits in a major field of study.

However, once these education majors graduate, they are woefully unprepared to teach in their subject field. For instance, a potential high school social studies teacher who earns a BA degree in Education will have *fewer units in social studies* than someone who earned an AA degree in social studies.

To make matters worse, these future teachers are then "credentialed" by enrolling in series of classes so inane that it nearly defies description.

In fact, it's no exaggeration to say that virtually all the success I enjoyed as a high school teacher can be attributed to *scrubbing from my mind everything I "learned" in those mind-numbingly useless teacher-credentialing classes.*

QUESTION 14

So, if "every profession has its failures", then how many bad teachers are there compared to other professions?

It all depends on your perspective.

Davis Guggenheim, producer of the documentary film *Waiting for Superman (2010)*, framed the issue this way:

Every year…

- *1 out of every 57* doctors loses his or her license to practice medicine.
- *1 out of every 97* lawyers loses his or her license to practice law.
- *1 out of every 1,000* teachers is fired for performance-related reasons.

In major urban centers such as New York City, Newark, Chicago, Los Angeles, Florida, Dallas, Tucson, and Des Moines, the statistics are *even worse* than those cited by Guggenheim.[124]

In New York City, New York:

- The *New York Daily News* reported that, "over the past three years [2007-2010], just *88 out of nearly 80,000* city schoolteachers have lost their jobs for poor performance."

---

124 http://teachersunionexposed.com/protecting.cfm. Accessed 11 September 2011.

- ❑ The Chancellor of New York City schools admitted that only *10 out of 55,000* tenured teachers were terminated during the 2006-2007 school year.

- ❑ In the entire state of New York, *only 17 tenured teachers* are terminated annually.

In Newark, New Jersey:

- ❑ Over a 10-year span, only about *47 out of 100,000* teachers were terminated from New Jersey's schools.

- ❑ Over a 4-year span, the Center for Union Facts (CUF) reported that Newark's school district only fired approximately *1 out of every 3,000* tenured teachers annually.

- ❑ Between the 2001-2002 and 2004-2005 school years, Newark's graduation rate—excluding diplomas "earned" through New Jersey's laughable remedial exams—*was just 30.6%.*

In Chicago, Illinois:

- ❑ According to *Newsweek*, one school district has failed miserably—*only 28.5%* of 11th graders met or exceeded expectations on Illinois standardized tests—and yet *only 0.1%* of the teaching staff were dismissed for performance-related reasons between 2005 and 2008.

- ❑ In other words, even though barely 1 in 4 students in 11th grade can read and do math, *only 1 in 1,000* teachers were deemed worthy of dismissal.

In Los Angeles, California:[125]

---

125 http://articles.latimes.com/2011/may/07/local/la-me-value-added-20110508. Accessed 11 September 2011.

- The *Los Angeles Times* reported in 2009 that *fewer than 2%* of teachers were denied tenure during the two-year probationary period after being hired.

- In fact, between 1995 and 2005, only *112 out of 43,000 (or 11 per year)* tenured teachers in Los Angeles faced termination.

- Keep in mind that in 2011, the Los Angeles Unified School District (LAUSD) had a *44% graduation rate*.

In Florida:

- According to scholar Richard Kahlenberg, the involuntary dismissal rate for teachers was an *abysmally low 0.05% "compared with 7.9 percent in the Florida workforce as a whole."*

In Dallas, Texas:

- Even when accounting for unofficial pressure to resign, *only 0.78%* of tenured teachers are terminated.

In Tucson, Arizona:

- During the past 5 years in Arizona, *only 7 out of 2,300* tenured teachers have been fired for classroom behavior.

In Des Moines, Iowa:

- During the last 5 years in the Des Moines school district, only *2 out of their 3,000* teachers have been fired for poor performance.

What possible explanation can justify these statistics? Why are teachers (apparently) *so much better than every other profession at keeping their jobs*?

Even more importantly, if we only consider the evidence we've examined thus far...*why aren't parents more confident in themselves?*

In fact, *why would any parent* believe that the edutocracy is better equipped than they are to decide what's best for their own children?

QUESTION 15

Why do teachers have such dramatically higher employee retention rates compared to other professions?

Well…it certainly helps (A LOT) that teachers' unions have negotiated tenure into their contracts…something conspicuously absent from non-public union employment.

- ❏ **An LAUSD superintendent admitted:** "Too many ineffective teachers are falling into tenured positions—the equivalent of jobs for life."[126]

- ❏ **USC education professor Julie Slayton acknowledged:** "It's [tenure] ridiculous and should be changed."[127]

- ❏ **In 2003, a Los Angeles union representative explained the problem best:** "If I'm representing them, it's impossible to get them out. It's impossible. Unless they commit a lewd act."[128]

Consequently, teachers' unions have made the process of firing *incompetent teachers with tenure* a prohibitively expensive and time-consuming process:[129]

---

126 http://www.nypost.com/p/news/opinion/opedcolumnists/ignorant_matt_H6uKjAXDP0G8p3qm2MdJHP. Accessed 10 January 2012.
127 http://www.realclearpolitics.com/articles/2011/08/05/schooling_matt_damon_110837.html. Accessed 1 September 2012.
128 http://people.ucsc.edu/~ktellez/hess_print.html. Accessed 5 September 2012.
129 http://www.teachersunionexposed.com/protecting.cfm. Accessed 5 September 2012.

- According to *Education Week*, during the 2006-2007 school year, New York City fired only *10 of its 55,000* tenured teachers. The cost of eliminating those teachers *averaged $163,142*. In New York State, the cost *averaged $128,941*.

- According to Scott Reeder of the *Small Newspaper Group*, the cost of eliminating tenured teachers *averaged $219,504* in just legal fees alone to advance a termination case past the union-supported hurdles.

- According the *Associated Press*, Columbus, Ohio's own president of the teacher's union admitted that firing a tenured teacher can cost *as much as $50,000*.

- According to their local press, a spokesman for Idaho school administrators confessed that districts have been known to spend *"$100,000 or $200,000"* in litigation costs just to eliminate a bad teacher.

Since union leaders can legally drag out termination proceedings for *months or even years* (during which time districts *must continue paying teachers, substitute teachers to replace them, and lawyers to arbitrate the proceedings*) the situation for students is unlikely to improve...*ever*.

Unfortunately, *school principals often serve as accomplices* of the teacher's unions in maintaining the practice of tenure.

In its analysis of Chicago's school district (typical among urban districts), the New Teacher Project[130] documented that *56% of principals admitted to inflating teacher ratings*.

---

130 http://tntp.org/assets/documents/TNTPAnalysis-Chicago.pdf?files/TNTPAnalysis-Chicago.pdf. Accessed 12 September 2012.

Yet, in evaluating the college-readiness for the state of Illinois' graduating class of 2014, the ACT Profile Report (2014) found:

- 62% were prepared in English Composition.
- 41% were prepared in Mathematics.
- 41% were prepared in Social Science.
- 35% were prepared in Biology.
- Only 26% were prepared in all four.

The reasons behind the inflated ratings are striking, and each can be directly traced back to the teacher's union contract:

- 30% of principals believe a teacher's dismissal would be prevented by tenure *regardless of the rating they were assigned*.

- 34% of principals believe enduring the lengthy union grievance proceedings to fire a teacher *isn't worth the hassle*.

- 51% of principals believe the union contract makes it *difficult to lower the rating* of a teacher that had previously received high ratings.

- 73% of principals believe that performance evaluations *fail to accurately evaluate performance*.

- Disturbingly, the New Teacher Project revealed that "between 2003 and 2006, *only nine teachers [out of the district's nearly 25,000]* received two or more 'unsatisfactory' ratings and none was dismissed."

How many private businesses in America would go bankrupt if their employees enjoyed the same level of job security that incompetent teachers have?

QUESTION 16

How do teachers themselves view tenure?

The surprising answer was revealed in a study conducted by Public Agenda (2003)[131] that polled 1,345 schoolteachers on a variety of education issues...*including tenure.*

In response to the question, "Does tenure mean that a teacher has worked hard and proved themselves to be very good at what they do?":

❏ **58% of the teachers responded that tenure "does not necessarily"** prove that teachers are good at what they do.

❏ **78% of the teachers admitted that at least some of their colleagues** "fail to do a good job and are simply going through the motions." [ouch]

The findings of Public Agenda (2003) were also confirmed by education author Terry Moe:[132]

❏ In response to the question, "Do you think tenure and teacher organizations make it too difficult to weed out mediocre and incompetent teachers?"...**55% of teachers, and 47% of union members, answered "yes."**

---

131 http://www.publicagenda.org/press-releases/americas-teachers-dont-make-us-scapegoats. Accessed 12 June 2009.
132 Terry M. Moe, *Special Interest: Teachers Unions and America's Public Schools* (Washington, DC: Brookings Institution Press, 2011).

So…IF *even a majority of teachers* acknowledge that tenure fails to promote professional excellence, then *why* do educrats and teachers' unions invest so much effort and money into protecting it?

AND if tenure is protecting the jobs of substandard teachers…how long are we willing to allow them to continue teaching our children?

Don't our children deserve better?

QUESTION 17

Even though educrats and teachers alike admit that other teachers are substandard, at least they still send their own children to government schools. Right?

Actually, the fact that large numbers of *public-school teachers and politicians* often choose to send *their own kids* to private schools instead of compulsory government schools...*basically exposes the "we support our public schools" rhetoric as complete nonsense.*

According to "Fwd: Where Do Public School Teachers Send Their Kids to School?" (7 September 2004), a study conducted by Brian Diepold, Denis P. Doyle & David A. DeSchryver for the Thomas B. Fordham Institute:

> "Teachers, it is reasonable to assume, care about education, are reasonably expert about it and possess quite a lot of information about the schools in which they teach. We can assume that **no one knows the condition and quality of public schools better than teachers who work in them every day.**"

Moreover, when significant numbers of public-school teachers choose to *send their own kids to private school over public school*...it makes quite an eye-opening statement about the "quality" of public schools in America.[133]

So...how many teachers send their kids to private school?

---

133 http://www.edexcellence.net/publications/publicteacherkids.html. Accessed 17 September 2012.

- 44% of public-school teachers in Philadelphia, PA.

- 41% of public-school teachers in Cincinnati, OH.

- 39% of public-school teachers in Chicago, IL.

- 38% of public-school teachers in Rochester, NY.

- 35% of public-school teachers in Baltimore, MD.

- 34% of public-school teachers in San Francisco/Oakland, CA.

- 33% of public-school teachers in New York City, NY.

- 29% of public-school teachers in Milwaukee, WI and New Orleans, LA.

- 28% of public-school teachers in Washington, DC.

- Nationally, 21% of public-school teachers, 37% of the U.S. House of Representatives[134] and 45% of the U.S. Senate[135] send their own children to private school...while *only 12% of the general public*[136] send their children to private school.

Two interesting conclusions can be drawn from the above data: (1) apparently, quite a few public-school teachers earn enough money to send their children to private schools and (2) with their "insiders" perspective, it's rather revealing that *significant numbers of those same teachers choose private schools over public schools for their own children.*

---

134 http://www.heritage.org/research/reports/2007/09/how-members-of-congress-practice-private-school-choice. Accessed 17 September 2012.
135 http://www.heritage.org/research/reports/2007/09/how-members-of-congress-practice-private-school-choice. Accessed 17 September 2012.
136 http://www.edexcellence.net/publications/publicteacherkids.html. Accessed 17 September 2012.

QUESTION 18

Given the comprehensive failure of compulsory government schooling, why hasn't Congress done something to constructively address these obvious problems?

Again, the problem can be traced back to the teacher's unions.

For decades, powerful teachers' unions have been *a major obstacle* to improving the compulsory government school system. And the National Education Association (NEA) and the American Federation of Teachers (AFT) are two of the *largest obstacles*.

In 1967, Sam Lambert, then-Executive Secretary of the NEA, openly declared the organization's intentions:

> "NEA will become **a political power second to no other special interest group**... NEA will have more and more to say about how a teacher is educated, whether he should be admitted to the profession, and whether he should stay in the profession."[137]

In 1972, Catherine Barrett, then-President of the NEA, reiterated Lambert's stated agenda:

---

[137] Samuel L. Blumenfeld, *NEA: Trojan Horse in American Education* (Phoenix, AZ: The Paradigm Company, 1985). Cf. James T. Bennett, *Tax-Funded Politics* (New Brunswick, NJ: Transaction Publishers, 2004).

"I believe we have arrived as professionals. We are **the biggest potential political striking force** in this country, and we are determined to **control the direction of education.**"[138]

The NEA's agenda remains unchanged and its dual obsession with *protecting teacher employment* and *expanding their political influence* continues to this day.

Although the NEA claims to be committed to "prepar[ing] every student to succeed", its leadership has (for decades) pursued decidedly different goals.

In 1982, Mary Hatwood Futrell, then-President of the NEA, candidly admitted that educating children is not their first priority:

> "The major purpose of our association is **not the education of children;** it is or ought to be the **extension and/or preservation of our members' rights**. We earnestly care about the kids' learning, but that is **secondary to the other goals**."[139]

Channeling the rhetoric of earlier NEA executives, Bob Chase, then-NEA President, flatly stated in 1997:

> "[NEA has] used our power to **block uncomfortable changes,** to **protect the narrow interest of its members,** and **not to advance the interests of students and schools**."[140]

---

138 Michael D. LeMay, *The Suicide of American Christianity* (Bloomington, IN: WestBow Press, 2012), "The Goals of the NEA."
139 Ed Remington, "Teachers Unions", *The Free Lance-Star* (1 Dec 1983). http://news.google.com/newspapers?nid=1298&dat=19831201&id=pGwQAAAAIBAJ&sjid=44sDAAAAIBAJ&pg=6865,6388. Accessed 3 February 2010.
140 David S. Broder, "So Much Talk about Better Education", *Washington Post* (16 February 1997). http://www.washingtonpost.com/wp-srv/politics/special/testing/stories/op021697.htm. Accessed 3 February 2010.

In 2009, Bob Chanin, retiring General Counsel of the NEA, reaffirmed these earlier sentiments when he clearly [re]stated the organization's purpose:

> "It is NOT because of our creative ideas. It is NOT because of the merit of our positions. It is NOT because we care about children. And it is NOT because we have a vision of a great public school for every child. NEA and its affiliates are effective advocates because we have power. And **we have power because there are more than 3.2 million people who are willing to pay us hundreds of millions of dollars in dues each year**, because they believe that we are the unions that can most effectively represent them." (emphasis added)

Chanin went on to conclude:

> "When all is said and done, NEA and its affiliates must never lose sight of the fact that **they are a union**, and what unions do **first and foremost is represent their members**."[141]

Albert Shanker, former President of the AFT and the United Federation of Teachers (UFT) famously sneered:

> "When school children start paying union dues, that's when I'll start representing the interests of school children."[142]

But even Shanker admitted that the government school system was broken:

---

141 Robert Chanin, "Bob Chanin Says Farewell", 2009 NEA Representative Assembly, New Orleans Convention Center, New Orleans (6 July 2009). Cf. http://www.youtube.com/watch?v=OwxiRXqH_hQ. Accessed 11 March 2011.
142 Walter E. Williams, *Do the Right Thing: The People's Economist Speaks* (Stanford, CA: Hoover Institution Press, 1995), p. 83.

"It's time to admit that public education operates like a planned economy, a bureaucratic system in which everybody's role is spelled out in advance, and there are few incentives for innovation and productivity. It's no surprise that our school system doesn't improve: It more resembles the communist economy than our own market economy."[143]

Apparently, as far as the teacher's unions are concerned, it isn't really "all about the kids."

In reality, teachers' unions are singularly focused on protecting their own...no matter how unqualified or incompetent those teachers may be for the job.

Shanker himself acknowledged that, *"a lot of people who have been hired as teachers are basically not competent."*[144]

Examined in its totality, political indifference to the comprehensive failure of compulsory government schooling is as baffling as it is infuriating...*until you follow the money*.

Considering the *incestuous relationship that exists between politicians and education special interests*, it is unlikely that meaningful change will ever inspire more than token congressional enthusiasm and support.

---

143 Interview with Albert Shanker, "Reding, Wrighting & Erithmatic", *Wall Street Journal* (2 October 1989).
144 Richard D. Kahlenberg, *Tough Liberal: Albert Shanker and the Battles Over Schools, Unions, Race, and Democracy* (New York, NY: Columbia University Press, 2007), p. 284.

❑ From 1990 to 2014, the education sector…which includes *teachers, professors, and administrators at primary/secondary schools, colleges, graduate schools, and vocational and technical institutes, but excludes teachers' unions…* contributed *$371,346,387 (2014 USD) to politicians and/or political campaigns* at the state and federal level.[145]

❑ From 1990 to 2014, the 3.2-million-member National Education Association (NEA), the 856,000-member American Federation of Teachers (AFT), and various other teachers' unions collectively contributed *$171,287,256 (2014 USD) to politicians and/or political campaigns* at the state and federal level.[146][147][148]

Put another way, from 1990 to 2014, these education special interest groups "invested" a *combined $542,633,643 (2014 USD) into politicians and/or political campaigns* at the state and federal level.

NOTE: Of the $543 million (2014 USD) that education special interest groups contributed to politicians and/or political campaigns at the state and federal level…*85% went to Democrats while 15% went to Republicans.*[149]

---

145 Center for Responsive Politics. Accessed 14 December 2011.
http://www.opensecrets.org/industries/totals.php?cycle=2010&ind=W04.
146 The membership of the NEA and the AFT makes them the largest and second-largest education unions in the United States, respectively. Additionally, the NEA is one of Education International's (EI-IE) 401 member organizations in 172 countries and territories, representing over 30 million education personnel from pre-school to university.
147 Center for Responsive Politics. Accessed 14 December 2015.
http://www.opensecrets.org/orgs/totals.php?cycle=2010&id=D000000064.
148 Center for Responsive Politics. Accessed 14 December 2015.
http://www.opensecrets.org/orgs/totals.php?cycle=2010&id=D000000083.
149 Center for Responsive Politics. Accessed 14 December 2015.
http://www.opensecrets.org/industries/totals.php?cycle=2010&ind=L1300.

QUESTION 19

Just what exactly did that $543 million (2014 USD) buy?

Apparently, the collective generosity of these education special interest groups purchased a protective congressional shield against overwhelming evidence of systemic and pedagogical incompetence…a sort of permanent "hall pass" absolving their responsibility in the matter.

Clearly, the edutocracy is *deeply invested in maintaining the status quo*. As the saying goes, "Money talks and BS runs the marathon."

At the National Education Association (NEA) convention in 1978, then-Executive Director Terry Herndon announced that:

> "The ultimate goal of the NEA is to tap the legal, political, and economic power of the U.S. Congress. [W]e want [NEA] leaders and staff with sufficient clout that they may roam the halls of Congress and **collect votes to reorder the priorities of the United States of America.**"[150]

So…nearly 40 years later…mission accomplished?

---

150 G. Gregory Moo, *Power Grab: How the National Education Association Is Betraying Our Children* (Washington, DC: Regnery Publishing Inc., 1999), p. 33.

QUESTION 20

Even though educrats have wasted...er...invested vast sums of money to "educate" primary and secondary school students, at least they've been prepared for college. Right?

Even if we completely ignore the national/international test scores and literacy rates we documented earlier, high school seniors looking ahead to college are *less prepared than ever*.

A comprehensive survey conducted by the *Chronicle of Higher Education (2006)*[151] polled 746 high school teachers and 1,098 college professors concerning the college readiness of their students.

The survey revealed that high school teachers consistently assessed their graduating seniors FAR more favorably than college professors assessed those same students as incoming freshmen.

In answering the question, *"How well prepared are your students for college-level work?"*, their responses varied significantly according to subject area:

❑ In evaluating their student's readiness for college-level Writing...*10% of high school teachers* and *44% of college professors* described those same students *"not well prepared."*

---

151 Alvin P. Sanoff, *Chronicle of Higher Education*, "A Perception Gap Over Students' Preparation" (10 March 2006).

- ❑ Conversely, only *36% of high school teachers* and *6% of college professors* described those same students as *"very well prepared."*

- ❑ In evaluating their student's readiness for college-level Mathematics…*9% of high school teachers* and *32% of college professors* described those same students as *"not well prepared."*

- ❑ Conversely, only *37% of high school teachers* and *4% of college professors* described those same students as *"very well prepared."*

- ❑ In evaluating their student's readiness for college-level Science, *38% of high school teachers* and *5% of college professors* described those same students as *"very well prepared."*

Overall, the survey revealed three key findings:

1. Only *35% of high school teachers* and *15% of college professors*, described their students as *"very well prepared"* for college.

2. A surprising *65% of high school teachers* and *84% of college professors*, described their students as *"somewhat prepared"* or *"unprepared"* for college.

3. Sadly, *12% of high school teachers* and *24% of college professors*, described their students as *"poorly prepared"* for college.

The findings of the Spellings Report (2006)[152] was published by a federal commission charged with examining the future of American higher education and confirmed the results of the *Chronicle of Higher Education (2006)* survey.

Their conclusions offered an even bleaker glimpse into the future:

- In 2007, *77% of the 1.3 million high-school graduates* who took the ACT examination were NOT PREPARED for college-level work in the core subjects of English, Mathematics, Reading, and Science.[153]

If the edutocracy is so determined to promote the idea that everyone needs to go to college…and high school is *not* preparing students to succeed in college…*then what exactly is it preparing students for?*

---

152 Marty Nemko, "College Degrees A Waste Of Time, Money," *The Tampa Tribune* (11 May 2008).
153 Marty Nemko, "College Degrees A Waste Of Time, Money," *The Tampa Tribune* (11 May 2008).

QUESTION 21

What explains this collective absence of academic preparedness?

Perhaps the answer can be found by examining what students do *with their time*.

An article published by *Science Daily (14 March 2008)*[154] at the American Heart Association's 48th Annual Conference on Cardiovascular Disease Epidemiology and Prevention reported:

- 60% of teens spend *20 hours per week* in front of a television or computer screen…or *1,040 hours per year*.

- 33% of teens spend *40 hours per week* in front of a television or computer screen…or *2,080 hours per year*.

- 7% of teens spend *50 hours per week* in front of a television or computer screen…or *2,600 hours per year*.

An article published by *The Daily Telegraph (10 February 2009)*[155] on a research survey conducted by Cybersentinel (a software solutions provider that allows parents to block access to certain sites) reported that:

- Teens spend an average of *31 hours a week* online or *1,612 hours per year*.

---

154 http://www.sciencedaily.com/releases/2008/03/080312172614.htm. Accessed 12 July 2011.
155 http://www.telegraph.co.uk/technology/4574792/Teenagers-spend-an-average-of-31-hours-online.html. Accessed 12 July 2011.

- Teens spend *3.5 hours a week* instant messaging their friends or *182 hours per year*.

NewsRx (5 February 2010)[156], reported on a research paper published by the Henry J. Kaiser Foundation entitled, "Daily Media Use Among Children and Teens Up Dramatically From Five Years Ago." Their findings concluded that:

- Teens spend an average of *7 hours and 38 minutes* on entertainment media per day or *2,786 hours per year*.

- Most of those hours consist of "media multitasking" (i.e., the use of multiple mediums) which means that teens are actually cramming a total of *10 hours and 45 minutes'* worth of media content into those *7 hours and 38 minutes*.

Based on these findings, since there are *8,760 hours in a year*, that would mean the average teenager spends...

- 2,920 hours of that year sleeping (33%).

- 2,786 hours of that year on media...movies, television, internet, texting, etc. (32%).

- 1,400 hours of that year at school (16%).

- 1,654 hours of that year...for everything else (19%).

NOTE: Read Mark Bauerlein's, *The Dumbest Generation: How the Digital Age Stupefies Young Americans and Jeopardizes Our Future (2008)* for a brilliant, if alarming, analysis of the impact that media and technology have on the lives of 14-24-year old's.

---

156 http://www.newsrx.com/health-articles/1747998.html. Accessed 12 July 2011.

QUESTION 22

After these academically unprepared products of media immersion are enrolled in college, what are they doing with their time?

Hint: it isn't studying.

A national survey of college freshmen, published by the Higher Education Research Institute (2001)[157], revealed that the amount of time high school students spends studying has steadily declined since 1987, when questions about the topic were first asked.

❑ In 1987, *53% of students* reported spending LESS THAN 6 hours per week on homework and studying.

❑ By 2001, *65% of students* reported spending LESS THAN 6 hours per week on homework and studying.

The National Survey of Student Engagement (NSSE)[158] defined class preparation as *"studying, reading, writing, rehearsing, and other activities related to your academic program"* and offered additional data to confirm this alarming trend:

---

157 L. J. Sax, A. W. Astin, W. S. Korn, & K. M. Mahoney, "The American Freshman: National Norms for Fall 2000", Higher Education Research Institute (Los Angeles, CA: University of California at Los Angeles, 2001).
158 Jeffrey R. Young, " Homework? What Homework? Students seem to be spending less time studying than they used to", *Chronicle of Higher Education* (6 December 2002). Cf.
http://chronicle.com/weekly/v49/i15/15a03501.htm. Accessed 11 December 2011.

According to college professors and administrators, students SHOULD spend at least *2 hours of class preparation for every hour spent in the classroom…or 25 to 30 hours per week* for a typical full-time student.

- However, *only 12% of freshmen* at four-year residential colleges reported spending 26 or more hours per week on class preparation…and *63% spend 15 or fewer hours.*

- *19% of full-time freshmen* admitted they spend only *1 to 5 hours per week* on class preparation…and seniors reported studying EVEN LESS.

- Students who created detailed logs of their study time *"discover[ed] that they spend a lot of time that doesn't add up to anything."*

- "Professors said that too many of their students are *more focused on grades rather than on learning."*

That must leave a warm-fuzzy in the heart of every parent who's made 18 years' worth of financial sacrifices for the ol' college fund.

QUESTION 23

Even if these students are not using their time studying, they must be learning something in their classes. Right?

It depends on how you define the word "something."

As physicist **J. Robert Oppenheimer (1904-1967)** wryly noted, *"No man should escape our universities without knowing how little he knows."*[159]

Columnist and author **J. Frank Dobie (1888-1964)** was even more blunt, *"The average Ph.D. thesis is nothing but a transference of bones from one graveyard to another."*[160]

The Founding Fathers understood that the liberties guaranteed by America's constitutional republic would ONLY endure IF its citizens retained a vital comprehension of our national principles.

Therefore, today's college students (i.e., our nation's future leaders) must understand our nation's historical legacy and founding principles if they are to become informed and engaged citizens. In other words, they must acquire "civic literacy."

---

159 http://quotes-lover.com/.
160 J. Frank Dobie, *A Texan in England* (Boston, MA: Little, Brown & Co., 1945).

In 2006, a joint commission[161] of the Intercollegiate Studies Institute (ISI), the National Civic Literacy Board (NCLB), and the University of Connecticut's Department of Public Policy (UConnDPP) published "The Coming Crisis in Citizenship: Higher Education's Failure to Teach America's History and Institutions."

Their report thoroughly documented the extent to which American colleges and universities (including some of our most elite schools) *have failed to improve their graduates' civic literacy.*

The ISI (2006) findings represented *the largest statistically valid survey ever conducted* to determine what colleges and universities are teaching their students about America's history and institutions.

UConnDPP administered *60 multiple-choice questions to 14,094 randomly selected students* (7,405 freshmen and 6,689 seniors) at 50 colleges and universities across the country to measure their knowledge in four subject areas:

1. American history
2. Government
3. America and the world
4. Market economy

Collectively, the ISI (2006) report provided a *"high-resolution image of collegiate education"* as it related to America's history and institutions on campuses throughout the nation. The results were deeply troubling and exposed nothing less than a *"looming crisis in American citizenship."*

---

161 http://www.americancivicliteracy.org/2006/summary.html. Accessed 13 October 2011.

To ensure that the content and administration of the American Civic Literacy Exam (2006) was statistically valid, six questions were included from the "Long-Term Trend U.S. History Assessment" administered by the National Assessment of Educational Progress (NAEP).

- Ironically, students (on average) scored HIGHER on the questions prepared by the ISI than on those prepared by the NAEP.

- Students who took the exam *did not complain that it was too difficult*, BUT frequently expressed dismay *their college education failed to prepare them better*, with *41% of seniors* stating that they were dissatisfied with their college program.

- Overall, freshmen scored an *average of 51.7% or "F-"* while seniors scored an *average of 53.2% or "F"*…a minimal improvement of 1.5%.

- Seniors at ALL 50 schools scored LOWER than 70%…or a "D" or "F".

- Seniors at 22 of the 50 schools scored LOWER than 50%…or an "F-".

- Seniors at 4 of the 50 schools scored LOWER than 40%…or whatever grade is lower than an "F-".

Despite receiving a college "education," seniors somehow failed to learn the fundamentals of America's history.

- 53.4% of seniors DID NOT KNOW the correct century when the first American colony was established at Jamestown.

- 55.4% of seniors DID NOT KNOW that Yorktown was the crucial battle that ended the American Revolution [28% chose Gettysburg (Civil War) as the correct answer].

Apparently, seniors were also kind of "iffy" on the importance of America's founding documents.

- 49.4% of seniors DID NOT KNOW that *The Federalist Papers* (foundational texts of America's constitutional meaning) were written to advocate ratification of the U.S. Constitution.

  [NOTE: seniors scored LOWER than freshmen on this question by 5.7%].

- 50%+ of seniors DID NOT KNOW that the Bill of Rights explicitly prohibits the establishment of an official religion for the United States.

- 72.8% of seniors DID NOT KNOW the source of the idea for "a wall of separation" between church and state.

- 75%+ of seniors DID NOT KNOW that the purpose of the Monroe Doctrine was to prevent foreign expansion in the Western Hemisphere.

Nor (apparently) did seniors learn much about current events.

- 45.2% of seniors DID NOT KNOW that the Ba'ath party was the primary source of Saddam Hussein's political support.

- 12.2% of seniors believed that the Communist Party was the primary source of Saddam Hussein's political support.

- 5.7% of seniors [insert gasp here] believed that Israel was the primary source of Saddam Hussein's political support.

These responses from *college seniors* clearly illustrate their *woefully inadequate knowledge of basic historical facts, ideas, and concepts* essential to meaningful participation in American civic life.

Remember [insert shudder here] that the nation's future leaders will be drawn from their ranks.

Alarmingly, several seniors actually scored LOWER than freshmen on the American Civic Literacy Exam (2006), a phenomenon termed "negative learning":

❑ Overall, *16 of the 50 schools* surveyed demonstrated negative learning.

❑ Sadly, most of the 16 schools that demonstrated negative learning were also highly ranked in the U.S. News & World Report's list of "Best colleges: 2011."[162]

Some of the other "highlights" from the ISI (2006) report included:

NOTE: All tuition costs are expressed in 2014 USD and DO NOT include room and board (on/off campus) or meal plans. Additionally, according to the National Center for Education Statistics (NCES), college students typically require an average of six years to graduate.

1. **Seniors at the University of Michigan**[163]—**which costs *$54,553 per year* and was ranked the *28th best school* in America by** *U.S. News & World Report*—*scored -0.1% lower than the freshmen*.

---

162 http://colleges.usnews.rankingsandreviews.com/best-colleges/national-universities-rankings/. Accessed 20 July 2011.
163 http://www.finaid.umich.edu/TopNav/AboutUMFinancialAid/Costof Attendance.aspx. Accessed 20 July 2011.

2. Seniors at Ithaca College[164]—which costs *$50,026 per year*—scored *-0.2% lower than the freshmen*.

3. Seniors at the University of Chicago[165]—which costs *$58,055 per year* and was ranked the *9th best school* in America by *U.S. News & World Report*—scored *-0.3% lower than the freshmen*.

4. Seniors at the Massachusetts Institute of Technology (MIT)[166]—which costs *$42,483 per year* and was ranked the *7th best school* in America by *U.S. News & World Report*—scored *-0.4% lower than the freshmen*.

5. Seniors at Williams College[167]—which costs *$46,793 per year*—scored *-0.7% lower than the freshmen*.

6. Seniors at the University of Florida[168]—which costs *$29,588 per year*—scored *-0.8% lower than the freshmen*.

7. Seniors at Wofford College[169]—which costs *$35,959 per year*—scored *-0.9% lower than the freshmen*.

8. Seniors at the University of Virginia[170]—which costs *$36,384 per year* and was ranked the *25th best school* in America by *U.S. News & World Report*—scored *-1.1% lower than the freshmen*.

---

164 http://www.ithaca.edu/catalogs/ug1011/studentinfo/expenses.php. Accessed 20 July 2011.
165 http://bursar.uchicago.edu/tuition.html#schedule. Accessed 20 July 2011.
166 http://web.mit.edu/facts/tuition.html. Accessed 20 July 2011.
167 http://web.williams.edu/admin/finaid/costs/. Accessed 20 July 2011.
168 http://www.sfa.ufl.edu/basics/cost-of-attendance/. Accessed 20 July 2011.
169 http://www.wofford.edu/businessoffice/tuition.aspx. Accessed 20 July 2011.
170 http://www.virginia.edu/financialaid/estimated.php#Undergrads. Accessed 20 July 2011.

9. Seniors at Georgetown University[171]—which costs $44,470 per year and was ranked the *21st best school* in America by *U.S. News & World Report—scored -1.2% lower than the freshmen.*

10. Seniors at Yale University[172]—which costs *$43,879 per year* and was ranked the *3rd best school* in America by *U.S. News & World Report—scored -1.5% lower than the freshmen.*

11. Seniors at State University of West Georgia[173]—which costs *$32,421 per year—scored -2.0% lower than the freshmen.*

12. Seniors at Duke University[174]—which costs *$43,960 per year* and was ranked the *9th best school* in America by *U.S. News & World Report—scored -2.3% lower than the freshmen.*

13. Seniors at Brown University[175]—which costs *$43,259 per year* and was ranked the *15th best school* in America by *U.S. News & World Report—scored -2.7% lower than the freshmen.*

14. Seniors at Cornell University[176]—which costs *$44,773 per year* and was ranked the *15th best school* in America by *U.S. News & World Report—scored -3.3% lower than the freshmen.*

---

171 http://finaid.georgetown.edu/coagrad.htm. Accessed 20 July 2011.
172 http://www.yale.edu/tuba/finaid/finaid-information/how-need-based-aid-works.html. Accessed 20 July 2011.
173 http://www.collegedata.com/cs/data/college/college_pg03_tmpl.jhtml?schoolId=1585. Accessed 20 July 2011.
174 http://admissions.duke.edu/jump/applying/finaid.html. Accessed 20 July 2011.
175 http://www.brown.edu/Administration/Admission/applyingtobrown/financialaid.html. Accessed 20 July 2011.
176 http://www.dfa.cornell.edu/dfa/treasurer/bursar/studentsparents/tuition. Accessed 20 July 2011.

15. Seniors at the University of California at Berkeley[177]—which costs *$40,453 per year* and was ranked the *22nd best school* in America by *U.S. News & World Report*—scored *-5.6% lower than the freshmen*.

16. Seniors at Johns Hopkins University[178]—which costs *$45,807 per year* and was ranked the *13th best school* in America by *U.S. News & World Report*—scored *-7.3% lower than the freshmen*.

The prestigious Carnegie Institution, whose selections are similarly respected by several nationally recognized organizations...mirrored the *U.S. News & World Report's* inexplicably generous college rankings.

According to the Carnegie Institution's own website:

> "The Classifications provide the framework in which institutional diversity in U.S. higher education is commonly described. It is now **the leading taxonomy of all accredited colleges and universities in the United States**, currently developed using nationally available data from the **U.S. Office of Postsecondary Education, the National Center for Education Statistics' Integrated Postsecondary Education Data System (IPEDS), the National Science Foundation, and the College Board**. The Carnegie Classifications™ have undergone multiple revisions, including changes in category names and definitions in 1976, 1987, 1994, 2000 and 2005, to reflect the shifting higher education universe. The 2010 update retains the same structure as the 2005 edition with few changes."

File this one under..."What an interesting coincidence?"

---

177 http://registrar.berkeley.edu/Default.aspx?PageID=feesched.html. Accessed 20 July 2011.
178 http://www.jhu.edu/finaid/prosp_stud_cost.html. Accessed 20 July 2011.

SO...the *same* gatekeepers whose *own* statistics demonstrate the mediocrity of government schools—*the U.S. Office of Postsecondary Education, the National Center for Education Statistics' Integrated Postsecondary Education Data System (IPEDS), the National Science Foundation, and the College Board*—are also *the most enthusiastic supporters* of the Carnegie Foundation's "Elite 108" selections? Hmm.

In fact, the following eleven institutions of "higher learning" featured in the ISI report (2006) that described the phenomena of "negative learning"...*are also included on the Carnegie Foundation's list of "Elite 108"*:

    3. University of Chicago (-0.3%)

    4. Massachusetts Institute of Technology (-0.4%)

    6. University of Florida (-0.8%)

    8. University of Virginia (-1.1%)

    9. Georgetown University (-1.2%)

    10. Yale University (-1.5%)

    12. Duke University (-2.3%)

    13. Brown University (-2.7%)

    14. Cornell University (-3.3%)

    15. University of California at Berkeley (-5.6%)

    16. Johns Hopkins University (-7.3%)

BOTTOM LINE: The inclusion of these eleven schools on the "Elite 108" represents either a *stunning lack of scrutiny*...or a *dreadfully deficient set of standards*.

QUESTION 24

So what is the explanation for this astonishing lack of basic civic knowledge?

The truth would likely trigger an insomnia epidemic...

Founded in 1995, the American Council of Trustees and Alumni (ACTA) is a 501(c)(3) nonprofit educational organization committed to academic freedom, excellence, and accountability and whose members are represented at over 400 colleges and universities.

In 2009, ACTA published a report, "What Will They Learn: A Report on the General Education Requirements at 100 of the Nation's Leading Colleges and Universities"[179] that investigated 100 major institutions of higher learning to determine whether seven key subjects were included in their general education requirements: (1) English Composition, (2) Literature, (3) Foreign Language, (4) U.S. History or Government, (5) Economics, (6) Mathematics, and (7) Science.

The results were...ah...*less than comforting*.

- ❏ NOT ONE single institution out of 100 required all seven subjects.

- ❏ 25 out of 100 institutions received an "F" for requiring ONE OR NO general education subjects.

---

179 http://www.goacta.org/publications/.../WhatWillTheyLearnFinal.pdf.

- 42 out of 100 institutions received a "D" or an "F" for requiring TWO OR FEWER general education subjects.

- 20 out of 100 institutions received a "C" for requiring THREE general education subjects.

- 33 out of 100 institutions received a "B" for requiring FOUR OR FIVE general education subjects.

- ONLY *5 out of 100* institutions received an "A" for requiring SIX general education subjects: (1) Brooklyn College of the City University of New York, (2) Texas A&M University, (3) University of Arkansas at Fayetteville, (4) United States Military Academy at West Point, and (5) University of Texas at Austin.

The American Council on Education (ACE), an organization established in 1918 and comprising more than 1,800 accredited, degree-granting colleges, universities, and higher education-related associations, organizations, and corporations similarly reported:[180]

- Only 15% of universities require tests for general knowledge.

- Only 17% of universities require tests for critical thinking.

- Only 19% of universities require tests for minimum competency.

So, what exactly have college seniors been prepared to do after graduation? It appears that colleges would rather not know the answer to that question…and are desperate to keep the public from finding out.

---

[180] http://www.creators.com/opinion/walter-williams/academic-dishonesty.html. Accessed 10 August 2011.

QUESTION 25

If these students aren't taking core general education courses, then what classes are they attending?

It sorta kinda depends on how you define "classes."

For instance, some of the colleges identified in ACTA's (2009) report permitted students to satisfy general education requirements with courses such as "Introduction to Popular TV and Movies" and "Science of Stuff." Still others sanctioned the study of "Bob Dylan" to satisfy a literature requirement and "Floral Art" to satisfy a natural science requirement.[181]

These are exactly the sort of silly classes you can find at www.socawlege.com. To find out just how silly, check out one of their articles entitled, "The 15 Most Ridiculous College Courses You Won't Believe Are Being Taught."[182]

Or you could go to the University of South Carolina [*tuition is just $40,178 (2014 USD) per year*] and take "Lady Gaga and the Sociology of Fame." Sociology professor Mathieu Deflem was inspired to develop the course after seeing the singer and artist on television, explaining to *The New York Times*, "The central objective is to unravel some of the sociologically relevant dimensions of the fame of Lady Gaga."

---

181 http://www.goacta.org/publications/.../WhatWillTheyLearnFinal.pdf.
182 http://socawlege.com/the-15-most-ridiculous-college-courses-you-wont-believe-are-being-taught/.

Or, if the Ivy-league is more your style, you could go to Cornell University [*tuition is just $44,773 (2014 USD) per year*] and take "Tree Climbing." This course will "teach you how to get up into the canopy of any tree, to move around, even to climb from one tree to another without touching the ground."

Finally, (and this is my personal favorite) you could go to Ivy-League icon Princeton University [*tuition is just $40,170 (2014 USD) per year*] and take "Getting Dressed." This course is taught by scholar and author Jenna Weissman Joselit and explores the art of getting ready in the morning by examining how what we wear—and why we wear it—shapes who we are, and vice versa.

FYE (For Your Entertainment): Click through an online catalogue of the politically-correct fluff courses offered at some of our "elite" universities…you will be both amused and saddened by what you find.

QUESTION 26

Even if the majority of classes that students take are silly electives, at least they learned something after six years of college. Right?

Unfortunately, *Americans of every demographic* are alarmingly uninformed about (1) our Constitution, (2) the functions of our government, (3) the key texts of our national history, and (4) basic economic principles...subjects long considered *essential for exercising our civic responsibility*.

In 2008, the ISI published "Our Fading Heritage: Americans Fail a Basic Test on Their History and Institutions"[183] which detailed the results from a *33-question basic civics survey administered to 2,508 adults* — including both *high school and college graduates* — to measure (1) the independent impact of college on the acquisition of civic knowledge, and (2) how a college education and civic knowledge independently influence a person's views.

- ❏ High school graduates average score = 44% (F-).

- ❏ College graduates average score = 57% (F+).

- ❏ Elected officials average score = 44% (F-) [gasp].

- ❏ Overall, *71% of the respondents failed the test* with an average score of 49% (F-).

---

183 http://www.americancivicliteracy.org/2008/summary_summary.html. Accessed 13 October 2011.

QUESTION 27

The ISI (2008) survey must have asked some pretty obscure questions for educated people to produce such poor results. Right?

It all depends upon what you consider obscure.[184]

- ❑ 30% of elected officials DID NOT KNOW that "life, liberty, and the pursuit of happiness" are the inalienable rights referred to in the Declaration of Independence.

- ❑ 45% of all respondents DID NOT KNOW Congress shares authority over U.S. foreign policy with the president and 25% incorrectly believed that Congress shares this power with the United Nations.

- ❑ 46% of college graduates DID NOT KNOW a basic description of the free enterprise system, in which all Americans participate.

- ❑ 47% of all respondents DID NOT KNOW the power to declare war belongs to Congress and 40% incorrectly believed that power belongs to the president. [*Between 2001-2008, Congress twice voted to approve foreign wars*].

- ❑ 51% of all respondents DID NOT KNOW all three branches of government...a minimal requirement for understanding America's constitutional system.

---

184 http://www.americancivicliteracy.org/2008/summary_summary.html. Accessed 13 October 2011.

- 73% of all respondents and 76% of college graduates DID NOT KNOW the Bill of Rights expressly prohibits establishing an official religion for the United States.

- 79% of all respondents DID NOT KNOW that the phrase "government of the people, by the people, for the people" was quoted from the Gettysburg Address.

- 80% of all respondents DID NOT KNOW the source for the phrase "a wall of separation" between church and state was from Thomas Jefferson's personal correspondence...with 49% incorrectly believing it can be found in the Constitution.

QUESTION 28

If these academically unprepared products of media immersion did not study, wasted their time taking silly electives, and their college degree failed to improve their "civic literacy"...then how do you explain the high GPA's of these graduates?

Actually, their academic performance only SEEMS to improve once these students graduate from high school and matriculate into college. *Cough* can you spell, "G-R-A-D-E I-N-F-L-A-T-I-O-N"? To put it bluntly, what is commonly labeled "grade inflation" is simply a euphemism for academic fraud.

Walter E. Williams, the brilliant professor of economics at George Mason University, perceptively identified this problem:

> "When a professor assigns a grade the student did not earn, it demonstrates **a lack of academic integrity.** When a university or college awards a degree to a student who has not mastered critical thinking skills, problem solving, and writing, it demonstrates **a lack of academic integrity.** Of course, perhaps the term 'fraud' does not accurately describe the problem. Apparently, **academic standards have fallen so low that ANYONE can now 'earn' A's and B's.**"[185]

Dr. Williams pointed out some rather "interesting coincidences" to consider:

---

185 http://www.creators.com/opinion/walter-williams/academic-dishonesty.html. Accessed 10 August 2011.

- Since the 1960s, college student academic achievement scores have plummeted, while their grade point averages (GPA) have skyrocketed.

- During the 1930s, the national average GPA at U.S. colleges and universities *was 2.35 (C+)*...TODAY the national average *GPA is 3.2 (B).*

- 80% of student grades given at the University of Illinois were "A's" and "B's".

- 50% of Columbia University students made the Dean's list.

- Only 6% of Stanford University students received "C's" ("D's" and "F's" had been previously banned).

Dr. Williams also warned that even the hallowed Ivy League was not immune from the disease of grade inflation:

- Harvard's grading practices have been termed, *"the laughingstock of the Ivy League."*

- 91% of Harvard University students were awarded honors during the spring graduation of 2001.

- One Harvard student admitted, *"I've coasted on far higher grades than I deserve. It's scandalous. You can get very good grades and earn honors, without ever producing quality work."*

Additionally, Dr. Harvey Mansfield, the William R. Kenan, Jr. Professor of Government at Harvard University since 1962, publicly criticized grade inflation at his institution saying:

> "There is something **inappropriate—almost sick**—in the spectacle of mature adults showering young people with unbelievable praise. We are **flattering our students** in our eagerness **to get their good opinion.** American colleges used to

set their own expectations. Now, increasingly, **they react to student expectations.**"[186]

Sadly, the above conclusions are substantiated by several additional sources that expand on the potential implications of rampant grade inflation.

The *Wall Street Journal* (30 January 1997) noted:

> "[A] bachelor of arts degree in 1997 **may not be the equal** of a graduation certificate from an academic high school in 1947."[187]

Dr. Perry Zirkel, Iacocca Professor of Education at Lehigh University declared:

> "…[grade inflation] is a societal trend to **de-emphasize competition** and **make people feel better about themselves.**"[188]

Arthur Levine, former president of the Woodrow Wilson National Fellowship Foundation and then-President Emeritus of the Teachers College at Columbia University stated:

> "The effect of grade inflation is a **devaluing of undergraduate degrees.**"[189]

Perhaps the *USA TODAY* headline from 21 November 2013 summed it up best, "College grade inflation: Does 'A' stand for 'average'?"

---

186 Harvey Mansfield, "Grade Inflation: It's Time to Face the Facts", *Chronicle of Higher Education* (2001).
187 http://econfaculty.gmu.edu/wew/articles/02/integrity.html. Accessed 10 August 2011.
188 http://www.newfoundations.com/Policy/Barndt.html. Accessed 10 August 2011.
189 Arthur Levine & Jeanette S. Cureton, "What We Know About Today's College Students" (1 March 1998).

Consider the following:[190]

- In 1969, *7% of all students* earned an "A-" or higher and *25% of all students* earned a "C" or less.

- By 1993, *26% of all students* earned an "A-" or higher and only *9% of all students* earned a "C" or less.

- In other words, between 1969 and 1993...students apparently became *257% "smarterer" and 67% "dumbless."*

These results are also corroborated by education researcher Brenda S. Sonner who reported that:[191]

- 28.3% of all college/university students earn "A's."

- 31.8% of all college/university students earn "B's."

- 21.5% of all college/university students earn "C's."

- 9.1% of all college/university students earn "D's."

- 9.3% of all college/university students earn "F's."

Henry Rosovsky, former Dean of the Faculty of Arts and Sciences, and Matthew Hartley, lecturer at the University of Pennsylvania's Graduate School of Education, published a two-year study on grade inflation at American colleges and universities that likewise confirmed these results and concluded:

---

190 Bradford P. Wilson, Executive Director, National Association of Scholars, address to Virginia Association of Scholars, Radford University (24 October 1998).
191 Brenda S. Sonner, *The Journal of Education for Business*, "A is for 'Adjunct': Examining Grade Inflation in Higher Education", Vol. 76 (January 2000), p. 5-8.

"…[a] compression in grades will create a system of grades in which A's predominate and in which letters (of recommendation) consist primarily of praise. **Meaningful distinctions will have disappeared.**"[192]

The report went on to document that although grade point averages have risen steadily over the past four decades, *student work has not improved nearly enough to justify such growth*.

---

192 http://www.amacad.org/multimedia/pdfs/publications/researchpapers monographs/Evaluation_and_the_Academy.pdf. Accessed 14 August 2008.

QUESTION 29

Grade inflation, though certainly alarming, cannot completely explain the scandalous decline in educational standards. So, what else could it be?

---

*Contrary to the famous cliché, cheaters apparently *do* prosper.*

The University of Missouri at Columbia daily newspaper reported:

> "According to research at the University's Center for Academic Integrity, **faculty are reluctant to act** on their suspicions of student cheating. A 1999 survey found that **one-third of faculty members** who knew of students cheating in their courses did nothing to address it. A recent survey of the MU faculty found that **51 percent of respondents** had ignored a suspected cheating incident."

One reason given:

> "...faculty members could be put on trial themselves."

One solution offered:

> "...the Academic Integrity Assessment Committee is considering an honor code... the honor code works quite well at some other universities."

Sadly, cheating is not confined to students. In fact, it seems this appalling absence of scholastic aptitude within the student body has tempted a number of college administrators to sell their academic souls in order to gain a favorable ranking in the *U.S. News & World Report*.

A few of their sins…both past and present:[194]

- ❑ Catherine Watt, former administrator at Clemson University, delivered a well-publicized presentation that explained how her institution addressed the "reputation" portion of the *U.S. News & World Report* survey, in which school officials are asked to assess the academic quality of peer undergraduate programs. Despite an *obvious conflict of interest*, the assessments of college administrators from *competing institutions* account for *25% of the ranking's formula*. Watt's presentation simply revealed how Clemson sought an edge by *rating competing schools as "below average."*

- ❑ The University of Miami *omitted scores of athletes and special admission students* to boost the SAT scores of incoming freshmen.

- ❑ At least one college mailed dollar bills to alumni with a request that they return them to the annual fund…thereby *inflating the number of alumni donors*.

- ❑ Baylor University asked students who had already been accepted into their school to re-take the SAT (hoping for higher scores) and offered to *compensate those students with a $300 bookstore credit*.

- ❑ Albion College reported a $30 alumni donation as a $6-per-year donation for five years in order to *increase the percentage of annual gifts from graduates over several years*.

---

194 Edward Fiske, "Gaming the College Rankings," *Minding the Campus*, Manhattan Institute (17 September 2009).

- ❏ The University of Southern California reported that 34 of its professors were members of a prestigious engineering association...though an investigation revealed that the number included people who had moved to industry or retired, while *only 17 were currently on staff and teaching.*

- ❏ The University of South Florida raised their students' collective SAT scores by simply *eliminating the bottom 6% of all scores.*

- ❏ Boston University raised its SAT scores by *excluding the verbal scores of foreign students—and including their math scores*—a practice believed to be rather common (sadly).

- ❏ Monmouth University improved its statistics by simply *adding 200 SAT points to its overall score.*

- ❏ In an exchange on the *Inside Higher Ed* website, a blogger from an unnamed northeastern university claimed, with absolute certainty, that the director of institutional research at his school had *forced the provost's resignation* by informing the president that *manipulated data had been sent* to *U.S. News & World Report.*[195]

Apparently, grade inflation, rampant cheating, and administrative malfeasance has become an "open secret" in academic circles.

In a recent progress report, former member of the Higher Learning Commission, Cecelia Lopez, revealed:

> "Since 1989, NCA [North Central Association] has made and continues to make a major commitment to the assessment of

---

[195] Middlebury College (Vermont) employed a director of institutional research and its provost was asked to resign in 2007. Coincidence?

student learning. The [Higher Learning] Commission's commitment proceeds from its belief that assessment of student academic achievement is key (1) to improving student learning, (2) to enabling an institution to verify that it is being accountable to its internal and external constituents, and (3) to documenting to the general public and interested parties the value of investing in higher education."[196]

It speaks volumes that the Higher Learning Commission *does not consider individual course grades to be valid measures of academic assessment*. Valid assessment measures include national tests, portfolios, senior seminar classes, and exit interviews...*but not grades*.

Colleges and universities are largely responsible for creating this knowledge deficit since the less that is expected and required of students, the fewer quality leaders will be produced.

Widespread academic corruption, particularly at the undergraduate level, does not bode well for the future of our nation. In fact, *most of the blame can be attributed to the boards of trustees* who must bear ultimate responsibility for the [mis]management of our colleges and universities.

In addition to the evidence already presented, it should be remembered that colleges and universities have a vested interest in *perpetuating the illusion of educational competency*.

As the late Frank Newman, former president of the Education Commission of the States and head of the Futures Project at Brown University admitted to *The New York Times*:

> "The real reason we don't test is, **we would rather not know**. We have a rhetoric about what we do. That rhetoric is: when

---

[196] http://www.endgradeinflation.org/. Accessed 21 July 2012.

you come to our institution you get a great liberal education, you're going to learn to think, you're going to learn about the life of the mind, you're going to learn the great traditions of Western thought.

If we start measuring, we will start finding out that **you didn't learn how to think, you didn't learn about the great traditions of Western thought**. Then we have a nasty little problem on our hands. If we find out that those students can't write well, **who do we turn to**?"[197]

---

197 Kate Zernike, "Tests Are Not Just for Kids," *New York Times* (4 August 2002). http://www.nytimes.com/2002/08/04/education/tests-are-not-just-for-kids.html?pagewanted=2. Accessed 14 October 2011.

QUESTION 30

Why go to college if grade inflation, cheating, and administrative corruption have become so rampant?

Permit me to answer that question with a question.

IF college students are spending *more time* than ever immersed in media…and *less time* than ever studying…

AND grades supposedly represent the knowledge they have acquired…

AND those grades have been proven to be wildly inflated…

AND many likely cheated to get those grades anyway…

AND American businesses spend $104 billion per year to "re-educate" graduates on what they should have learned in college…

THEN what exactly is a college degree…*even an expensive one*…worth?

QUESTION 31

Even though the current cohort of America's college graduates are looking at mediocre in the rear-view mirror, at least they're doing better than previous generations. Right?

Unfortunately, our future leaders will be *comprehensively less informed* than ever before.

A 2002 survey published by the National Association of Scholars (NAS) discovered that:

> "Contemporary **college seniors scored little or no higher than the high-school graduates of a half-century ago** on a battery of 15 questions assessing general cultural knowledge. The questions, drawn from a survey originally done by the Gallup Organization in 1955, covered literature, music, science, geography, and history."[198]

The overall average percentage of correct responses for Gallup's survey (1955) was:

❏ 53.5% correct for today's college seniors.

❏ 54.5% correct for 1955 high school graduates.

❏ 77.3% correct for 1955 college graduates.

---

[198] "Today's College Students Barely More Knowledgeable than High School Students of 50 Years Ago, Poll Shows", Zogby International (18 December 2002).

Stephen H. Balch, president of the National Association of Scholars (NAS), noted:

> "The results, though somewhat mixed and based on a limited number of questions, are hardly reassuring. **America has poured enormous amounts of tax dollars** into expanding access to higher learning. Students spend, and pay for, **many more years in the classroom than was formerly the case.**
>
> "Our evidence suggests that this time and treasure may **not have substantially raised student cultural knowledge above the high school levels of a half-century ago.** Worse yet, the high cultural interest and aspirations of today's college seniors are neither consistently nor substantially more elevated than yesteryear's secondary school graduates.
>
> "Creating such interests and aspirations has traditionally been considered a core element of the collegiate experience. If the last fifty years have in fact witnessed few gains in this respect, it represents **a real disappointment of once widespread hopes.**"[199]

Our future leaders are in full intellectual retreat and seem incapable of reversing their present trajectory any time soon.

According to an October 2002 report released by the National Center for Postsecondary Improvement (NCPI) at Stanford University:

> "Globalization necessitates that colleges and universities prepare their students to be citizens of the world, who understand the serious challenges of competitiveness and interdependence that come in its wake.

---

[199] "Today's College Students Barely More Knowledgeable than High School Students of 50 Years Ago, Poll Shows", Zogby International (18 December 2002).

Globalization also prompts institutional leaders and policymakers alike to rethink their reach and their boundaries…

…a focus that has become increasingly salient as the World Trade Organization defines the extent to which distributed education is to be a freely traded good."[200]

Though preparing students for the reality of global interdependence has some merit, *it is far more alarming that*:

"…higher education's performance for the most part has **fallen short of fostering an engaged citizenry**… Recent evidence indicates that **today's college graduates are actually less engaged in the civic life of the nation than were preceding generations**."[201]

---

200 http://www.stanford.edu/group/ncpi/documents/pdfs/beyond_dead_reckoning.pdf. Accessed 11 November 2011.
201 http://www.endgradeinflation.org/. Accessed 11 November 2011.

QUESTION 32

Is the reason that students are substandard in basic skills like reading and writing because so many of them graduate with academic deficiencies and mediocre literacy rates?

Um...yeah...like totally.

In 2003, the National Commission on Writing in America's Schools and Colleges reported:[202]

❑ Writing ability among students is "bad."

❑ C. Peter Magrath, commission chair and president of the National Association of State Universities and Land Grant Colleges, described this situation "a very serious matter for our society."

❑ The commission described writing as the "forgotten r," but mathematics scores were no better and reading ability was termed "a threat to this society."

---

[202] C. Peter Magrath & Arlene Ackerman, "The Neglected 'R': The Need for a Writing Revolution", National Commission on Writing in America's Schools and Colleges (April 2003).
http://www.collegeboard.com/prod_downloads/writingcom/neglectedr.pdf.

The National Center for Postsecondary Improvement (NCPI) at Stanford University, cited previous reports to support their conclusions concerning this alarming trend:[203]

- The National Commission on Excellence in Education, "A Nation at Risk" (1983) report that "focused on the declining quality of learning in the nation's primary and secondary schools..."

- The National Commission on Excellence in Education, "Involvement in Learning: Realizing the Potential of American Higher Education" (1984), a report considered, "perhaps the most influential...", identified "the need for higher academic expectations, enhanced student involvement, and for the assessment of learning."

Consequently, many Americans, even college-educated ones, are at or below basic literacy levels.

According to studies published by the U.S. Department of Education, Institute of Education Sciences, National Center for Education Statistics, National Adult Literacy Survey (1992), and the National Assessment of Adult Literacy (2003):[204]

Evaluation standards were divided into four categories:

- "Below Basic" = no more than the most simple and concrete literacy skills.

- "Basic" = skills necessary to perform simple and everyday literacy activities.

---

203 National Center for Postsecondary Improvement (NCPI) "Beyond Dead Reckoning: Research Priorities for Redirecting American Higher Education," U.S. Department of Education Office of Educational Research and Improvement (Palo Alto, CA: Stanford University, October 2003).
204 http://nces.ed.gov/naal/. Accessed 13 October 2011.

- "Intermediate" = skills necessary to perform moderately challenging literacy activities.

- "Proficient" = skills necessary to perform more complex and challenging literacy activities.

The results were…shall we say…*disappointing to say the least*.

- In 1992, 52% of high school graduates, 16% of college graduates, and 45% of adults were, "*at or below basic*."

- But by 2003, 53% of high school graduates, 19% of college graduates, and 44% of adults were "*at or below basic*."

In fact, according to the Spellings Report (2006)[205], college graduates are struggling more than ever:

- "Over the past decade, *literacy among college graduates has actually DECLINED*."

- 40%+ of college freshmen at four-year institutions *DO NOT graduate in six years*.

BOTTOM LINE: Even *among college graduates*, literacy rates are falling, and their writing skills are declining even faster.

So…shud we b wureed?

---

205 Marty Nemko, "College Degrees A Waste Of Time, Money," *The Tampa Tribune* (11 May 2008).

QUESTION 33

What happens when these college graduates enter the marketplace?

Let's just say that a college degree isn't exactly the equivalent of winning a Golden Ticket into Willie Wonka's chocolate factory.

Today's college graduates are being turned loose into the "global marketplace" less prepared than ever. In 2011, *about 1.5 million, or 53.6%, of bachelor's degree-holders under the age of 25 were jobless or underemployed*, the highest share in 11 years.[206]

According to the National Center of Education Statistics:

❏ Employers reported that *many college graduates lack the basic skills of critical thinking, writing, and problem solving*. Some employers have even hired English and math tutors to teach their employees how to write memos and perform simple computations.[207]

As a result, employers are being forced to select their prospective employees from an increasingly substandard labor pool.

A special joint report by *The Chronicle of Higher Education* and *American Public Media's Marketplace* (4 March 2013) found that

---

[206] http://www.huffingtonpost.com/2012/04/22/job-market-college-graduates_n_1443738.html. Accessed 23 August 2012.
[207] http://nces.ed.gov/naal/. Accessed 13 October 2011.

approximately half of the 704 employers who participated in the study said *they had trouble finding recent college graduates qualified to fill positions at their company.*

Sadly, these results are hardly surprising and are corroborated in a study funded by the Pew Charitable Trusts (2006):[208]

- *50% of college seniors scored below "proficient" levels* on a test requiring them to perform basic tasks such as understand the arguments of newspaper editorials or compare credit-card offers.

- Nearly *20% of college seniors possessed only basic quantitative skills* such as estimating whether their cars had enough gas to refill their tanks at the gas station.

The ACTA (2009) report reinforces the earlier conclusions of both the Pew (2006) and Spellings (2006) reports stating that:

> "Even as our students need broad-based skills and knowledge to succeed in the global marketplace, **our colleges and universities are failing to deliver.**

---

208 Marty Nemko, "College Degrees A Waste Of Time, Money," *The Tampa Tribune* (11 May 2008). Dr. Marty Nemko was named "The Bay Area's Best Career Coach" by the *San Francisco Bay Guardian*. He has served as a consultant to 15 college presidents and holds a Ph.D specializing in the evaluation of education from the University of California, Berkeley, and has subsequently taught there. His five published books include, *The All-in-One College Guide: A Consumer Activist's Guide to Choosing, Getting Into, Finding the Money For, and Making the Most of College*, and *Cool Careers for Dummies (3rd edition)*, rated the #1 most useful college guide by the Readers Choice poll.
209 http://www.goacta.org/publications/.../WhatWillTheyLearnFinal.pdf.

"Topics like U.S. government or history, literature, mathematics, and economics have become mere options on far too many campuses. Not surprisingly, **students are graduating with great gaps in their knowledge—and employers are noticing.**"[209]

After entering the marketplace, college graduates are discovering firsthand the devasting consequences of *low course standards, grade inflation, and cheating*.

As *The Christian Science Monitor* **reported back in 2001:**

"Once graduates enter the job market, they discover they can't bank on those **undeserved grades.**"[210]

The damaging effects of *low standards, grade inflation, and cheating* has not gone unnoticed by American corporations and they have responded by becoming increasingly involved in educational reform at the nation's public schools.

At the 2001 National Education Summit, Louis V. Gerstner Jr., former CEO and chairman of the board of IBM observed:

"[J]ust as the Founding Fathers understood, that absent a healthy, vital system of free public education you can't have an enlightened electorate, which means **you can't sustain a working Democracy; you can't build a competitive workforce, which means you can't envision a more prosperous future.** It's exactly that clear cut.

"We have an abiding responsibility to the kids and their future."

---

210 Staff, *The Christian Science Monitor*, "Licking Grade Inflation" (6 November 2001).

Dr. Craig Barrett, then-president and CEO of Intel Corporation, addressed the issue of educational standards in his speech "Failure is not an Option: Solving the Math-Science Crisis in our Schools" (November 2001), one in a series entitled, "Profiles of Excellence in Business and Education Leadership" produced by the National Alliance of Business:

> "In our graduate schools, **about half of engineering Ph.D.'s— and almost as many math and computer science doctorates— are earned by foreign nationals.** Colleges are recruiting these foreign students because **so few U.S. students are interested in these advanced degrees or have the math and science background to succeed in these programs.**
>
> "Yet, even with these foreign students, the numbers of electrical engineers, computer engineers, and systems engineers graduating from our universities have **declined by 20 percent.**
>
> "This low achievement (in math and science scores) is not the fault of individual students, teachers or administrators, but evidence of **fundamental flaws in our national system of teaching and learning**... we must persevere and **completely change our system of teaching and learning** from what we have done in the past.
>
> "Every year we debate these topics or provide inadequate resources to produce real change, we lose another graduating class and **condemn those children to a lower level of professionalism in their careers.**"

But even among college graduates who manage to land a job, their employers routinely complain that they lack the requisite writing and analytical skills necessary to succeed in the workplace.

- ❑ The National Center for Education Statistics (NCES) reported that *only 31% of college graduates can read and understand a complex book*.[211]

- ❑ According to a 2006 joint survey conducted by the Conference Board, Corporate Voices for Working Families, the Partnership for 21st Century Skills, and the Society for Human Resource Management, *only 24% of employers believed graduates of four-year colleges were "excellently prepared" for entry-level positions*.[212]

- ❑ In 2009, corporations and government organizations in North America *spent approximately $104.3 billion*—or between 1.5 to 2% of their operating expenses—*on training products and services* [read: stuff that college graduates failed to learn at their expensive institutions of higher learning].[213]

Americans increasingly understand that the *costs of higher education often exceed the perceived benefits*.

For instance, imagine that you're the CEO of a Fortune 500 company and need to hire an investment manager. You narrow all of the applicants down to two potential candidates:

Candidate No. 1…graduated *summa cum laude* from Harvard University and holds an MBA from the Wharton School of Business.

- VS-

Candidate No. 2…never graduated from college, but instead spent the last eight years being personally mentored by Warren Buffett (net worth: $65+ billion) in investing.

---

211 Sam Dillon, "Literacy Falls for Graduates From College, Testing Finds," *New York Times* (16 December 2005).
212 Walter Williams, "What Will They Learn?," *JewishWorldReview.com* (26 August 2009).
213 Doug Harward, "How Big is the North America Training Market?," *TrainingIndustry.com* (29 December 2009).

Who would you hire to manage the company's money?

Not to belabor the point but consider the following list of those who have successfully navigated the road to success WITHOUT a college degree.

[NOTE: The list represents a non-exhaustive abridged version that excludes "honorary" degrees]:

Political figures...

- Founding Father Benjamin Franklin... U.S. Presidents George Washington, Andrew Jackson, Martin Van Buren, William Henry Harrison, Zachary Taylor, Millard Fillmore, Abraham Lincoln, Andrew Johnson, Grover Cleveland, and Harry S. Truman... revolutionary Malcolm X... former Governor [MN] Jesse Ventura... former Israeli president David Ben Gurion... Eleanor Roosevelt...

Business magnates...

- Microsoft co-founder Bill Gates... Dell founder Michael Dell... Apple co-founder Steve Wozniak... IBM founder Thomas Watson... Domino's founder Tom Monaghan... Wendy's founder Dave Thomas... Blockbuster Video founder and owner of the Miami Dolphins Wayne Huizenga... McDonald's founder Ray Kroc... Oracle founder Larry Ellison... Ford Motor founder Henry Ford... cosmetics pioneer Helena Rubenstein... CNN founder Ted Turner... Disney founder Walt Disney... Mrs. Field's founder Debbie Fields... DreamWorks co-founder David Geffen... NBC mogul David Sarnoff... Standard Oil founder John D. Rockefeller... U.S. steel co-founder Andrew Carnegie... fashion designer Coco Chanel... Pritikin Diet creator Dr. Nathan Pritikin... celebrity chef Wolfgang Puck...

Inventors & architects...

- Inventor Alexander Graham Bell... inventor Thomas Edison... airplane inventors Wilbur and Orville Wright... architect Frank Lloyd Wright... architect Buckminster Fuller...

Journalists & media personalities...

- *PBS* NewsHour's Nina Totenberg... *ABC* anchorman Peter Jennings... *CBS* anchorman Walter Cronkite... radio personality Rush Limbaugh... satirist H. L. Mencken...

Actors, directors, musicians, & sports figures...

- Actress/singer Barbra Streisand... actor Tom Hanks... entertainer Ellen DeGeneres... actor/director Woody Allen... actor Warren Beatty... musician Bob Dylan... actor Leonardo DiCaprio... actress Sally Field... actress Jane Fonda... director Quentin Tarantino... folksinger Joan Baez... actor Dustin Hoffman... actor/director Robert Redford... entertainer Rosie O'Donnell... singer Madonna... tennis legend Martina Navratilova...

Writers...

- Poet Maya Angelou... author William Faulkner... author Jane Austen... author Alex Haley... author Ernest Hemingway... anthropologist Richard Leakey...

FYE (For Your Entertainment): The website www.collegedropoutshalloffame.com offers a comprehensive list of successful people who never graduated from college.

QUESTION 34

Since we can look forward to being governed by substandard leaders, how will large-scale educational ignorance—and the academic dishonesty that supports it—affect our country?

One distinguished historian offers a chilling answer.[214][215]

David McCullough, 2002 Pulitzer Prize-winning author and former president of the Society of American Historians, warned the Senate Committee on Health, Education, Labor, and Pensions that widespread ignorance of American history among students and teachers at high schools and colleges represents a major threat to the nation's security.

He lamented that, *"we are raising a generation of people who are historically illiterate"* and ignorant of the basic philosophical foundations of America's constitutional free society. McCullough cautioned that the consequences of this national ignorance will be catastrophic stating:

> "**We can't function as a society if we don't know who we are and where we came from.** For a free, self-governing people, **something more than a vague familiarity with history is essential** if we are to hold onto and sustain our freedom."

---

214 George Archibald, "McCullough calls national 'amnesia' threat to liberty", *The Washington Times* (16 May 2003), p. 1.
215 Ernest W. Lefever, "Ignorance of recent events endangers America: students today are failing U.S. history. But more important, they will fail the nation in the future unless this trend is reversed," *VFW Magazine* (September 2003).

According to McCullough, there are presently ONLY THREE colleges in the United States whose graduation requirements include a course on the U.S. Constitution: (1) the U.S. Military Academy at West Point, (2) the Naval Academy at Annapolis, and (3) the Air Force Academy in Colorado Springs.

This de-emphasis of the Constitution and basic American history has produced *a level of ignorance that is truly staggering in its enormity*. For example, when high school students were asked to identify the commanding general of the American revolutionary troops at Yorktown who accepted the surrender of British General Charles Cornwallis:

- 50%+ guessed Ulysses S. Grant [Commanding General of *the Union Army during the Civil War*].

- 6% guessed Douglas MacArthur [Supreme Allied Commander of *the South Pacific theater during World War II*].

McCullough added that when there are students at Ivy League colleges who think that *Germany and Japan were American allies during World War II, the nation has a very serious problem*.

Or, perhaps the answer is simply that you cannot learn what you do not read or are not taught.

In a report published by ACTA (2002), researchers Ann Neal & Jerry Martin found that:

> "...**none** of the nation's top 50 colleges and universities require students to study American history and **only 10% require students to study history at all**."[216]

Sadly, McCullough is not alone in his dismal predictions.

---

216 Ann Neal & Jerry Martin "Restoring America's Legacy", American Council of Trustees and Alumni (September 2002).

The methodology employed by institutions of higher learning to self-evaluate their progress only compounds an already troubling situation. Universities *value inputs over outputs* in their calculations (e.g. per-capita expenditures, the ethnic diversity of the student body and faculty, the number of volumes in the library, and class size). Basically, they care about *everything except what students actually learn*.

In 2004, the American Association of Colleges and Universities (AAC&U) issued a report that found higher education's assessment of outcomes was:

> "...spotty [and there was] no national data [that assessed] civic responsibility and engagement."[217]

A 2005 report published by the AAC&U goes even further:

> "...the most important outcomes of college study—outcomes widely regarded as key to economic opportunity and democratic citizenship—have been **insufficiently addressed** in reliable, cumulative assessments of students' gains from their college studies.
>
> "For all the value society places on the kinds of learning addressed in this report, we still **lack persuasive evidence about how well today's students are actually doing**."[218]

Former Harvard University president Derek Bok, in his eye-opening book, *Our Underachieving Colleges (2006)* **warned:**

---

[217] http://www.epi.soe.vt.edu/perspectives/policy_news/pdf/civicliteracy.pdf. Accessed 12 July 2011.
[218] http://www.aacu.org/advocacy/pdfs/leap_report_final.pdf.

"The American Political Science Association Task Force on Civic Education...has declared it 'axiomatic that current levels of political knowledge, political engagement, and political enthusiasm are so low as to **threaten the vitality and stability of democratic politics in the United States.**'"[219]

Moreover, this lack of basic political knowledge has serious consequences as evidenced by a survey conducted by Rasmussen Research/Portrait of America (1999):[220]

❑ Only 49.5% of respondents would *vote for* passage of the U.S. Constitution if it were presented in ballot form today, 23% percent would *vote against it*, and 27% *were unsure* if they would support it.

In another survey jointly conducted by Rasmussen Research/Portrait of America (2000):[221]

❑ 35% of respondents believed that eliminating the Second Amendment from the U.S. Constitution and making personal firearms ownership unlawful would make the nation safer, 42% believed that would make the nation more dangerous, and 16% believed that would have no impact on safety.

❑ Only *36% of respondents* believed Congress should follow the U.S. Constitution.

---

219 Derek Bok, *Our Underachieving Colleges: A candid look at how much students learn and why they should be learning more* (Princeton, NJ: Princeton University Press, 2006).
220 http://www.worldnetdaily.com/bluesky_dougherty/20000725_xnjdo_only _half_.shtml. Accessed 5 September 2012.
221 http://www.worldnetdaily.com/bluesky_dougherty/20000725_xnjdo_only _half_.shtml. Accessed 5 September 2012.

- 48% of respondents believed that the federal government routinely ignores its constitutional limitations while only 35% believe the federal government operates within the U.S. Constitution.

- Only *51% of respondents would vote to pass the U.S. Constitution* if it were presented in ballot form today, 22% percent would vote against it, and 27% were unsure if they would support it.

- 51% of respondents believed Congress should pay for 100,000 additional teachers in local school districts even though there is no constitutional authority to provide such funding.

- 53% of young adults and 45% of women preferred to support art funding even if unauthorized by the U.S. Constitution.

- Though 56% of respondents believed following the U.S. Constitution was the best way to run our country, 37% believe it should be updated to "reflect major societal changes of the past 200 years."

- 63% of respondents believed that Congress uses the U.S. Constitution as an excuse to ban school prayer.

- 64% of respondents would modify the U.S. Constitution to grant LESS power to Congress, while 12% would grant MORE power to Congress.

- 81% of respondents believed that First Amendment protections of freedom of speech generally benefit the nation while 7% disagree.

One result of this shocking ignorance was noted by former Harvard University president Derek Bok, who ruefully observed:

"[T]he dominant feature of nonvoting in America is **lack of knowledge about government**; not distrust of government, lack of interest in politics, lack of media exposure to politics, or feelings of inefficacy."[222]

Thomas Jefferson once remarked, *"If a nation expects to be ignorant and free...it expects what never was and never will be."*

The freedom that Jefferson spoke of is imperiled by a growing illiteracy of America's heritage...as evidenced by our collective historical amnesia.

It is crucial for the future prosperity (and longevity) of our nation that today's college students [read "our nation's future leaders"] become sufficiently grounded in America's history and founding principles.

Higher education must do more than simply produce expensive degrees for display on an office wall; it must produce informed and engaged citizens who can assume the larger responsibility of guiding America and raising the next generation.

As the Framers completed the task of establishing our constitutional republic, several departed Philadelphia for their respective home states and helped establish colleges and universities designed to cultivate leaders for the nation's future. The Framers understood that free people are not born...they are educated.

Dr. Benjamin Rush, signatory to the Declaration of Independence, noted:

---

[222] Derek Bok, *Our Underachieving Colleges: A Candid Look at How Much Students Learn and Why They Should Be Learning More* (Princeton, NJ: Princeton University Press, 2006), p. 176.

"The business of education has acquired a new complexion by the independence of our country. The form of government we have assumed, has created a new class of duties to **every American.**"[223]

Two centuries later, serious concerns exist that our colleges and universities *no longer provide even the basics of American civics*. Perhaps the previous statistics should come as no surprise considering that so many institutions of "higher learning" sanction general education standards that *do not require the study of U.S. History/Government*.

Students and their parents continue to pay exorbitant sums of money to acquire a nominal (at best) education while the knowledge deficit continues to grow at a dizzying pace.

As Justice José A. Cabranes of the U.S. Court of Appeals for the Second Circuit, wisely noted:[224]

> "Future leaders needed to know **the history and ideas that had shaped the West** in order for our country to protect itself and to pursue its ideals…[r]eadings from the great texts of the West would provide **the necessary background** for whatever political, ideological, or intellectual struggles lay ahead."

Cabranes believes this could be accomplished by a coherent core general education requirement that reflected:

> "…a series of choices—the choice of the lasting over the ephemeral; the meritorious over the meretricious; the thought-provoking over the merely self-affirming.

---

[223] http://press-pubs.uchicago.edu/founders/print_documents/v1ch18s30.html. Accessed 2 September 2011.
[224] José A. Cabranes, "Essays in Perspective Fostering Judgement: Sixty Years of Well-Directed Studies", Institute for Effective Governance (Fall 2006), Vol. 4.

"[An appropriate general education curriculum] ensure[s] that their studies—and their lives—**are well-directed**."

The edutocracy would do well to heed the judge's sage advice.

Today, the "American Success Story" script encourages parents to ensure their kids get good grades (1) in elementary school to get into the right middle school, (2) in middle school to get into the right high school, (3) in high school to get into the right college, and (4) in college to get a good job, get married, have 2.4 children, and live happily ever after in a house with a white-picket fence.

BUT, contrary to the conventional wisdom that a college degree represents the apex of human achievement, there are strong indications that *Americans have begun to question its value*.

According to a national Zogby-Scoop44 Poll (18-20 August 2009), that surveyed 2,530 likely voters:

- Only 53% of ALL respondents stated that a college degree IS worth the price.

- *But*...33% of ALL respondents, 25% of ALL college graduates, and 56% of ALL non-graduates stated that a college degree IS NOT worth the price.

- Only 55% of respondents ages 18-29, stated that a college degree IS worth the price.

- *But*...35% of ALL respondents, 28% of college graduates, and 41% of non-graduates ages 18-29, stated that a college degree IS NOT worth the price.

It's rather telling that *30% of college graduates* and *45% of non-graduates ages 65+* believe that a college degree IS NOT worth what it costs.

QUESTION 35

Why does "higher education" cost so much money when it produces such poor results?

The answer is difficult to accept because even as the quality of "higher education" continues to plummet, the cost continues to skyrocket.

According to data compiled by the National Center for Education Statistics (NCES), *from 1970 to 2014*:[225]

❏ The average cost of tuition + room and board at *4-year public universities* soared from $1,552 (2014 USD) to $22,598...*an increase of 1,356%!*

❏ The average cost of tuition + room and board at *4-year private universities* soared from $3,323 (2014 USD) to $31,231...*an increase of 840%!*

To further illustrate the rapidly escalating cost of tuition, consider the University of Pennsylvania (UPenn), a private research university located in Philadelphia, Pennsylvania.[226] [227]

This elite school is one of the Colonial Colleges, a member of the Ivy League, and the fourth-oldest institution of higher education in the United States.

---

225 https://nces.ed.gov/programs/digest/d07/tables/dt07_320.asp
226 http://www.sfs.upenn.edu/tuition/Undergrad-2011-2012.htm. Accessed 27 October 2011.
227 http://www.archives.upenn.edu/histy/features/tuition/1950.html. Accessed 27 October 2011.

Originally founded by Benjamin Franklin in 1740, UPenn is one of fourteen founding members of the Association of American Universities.

In 1900, tuition + room and board for the University of Pennsylvania was $4,200 (2014 USD) per year. By 1950, the cost had risen to $6,100 (2014 USD), and by 2014 it had skyrocketed to $45,600. *In other words...*

- From 1900 to 1950, the cost increased by *a modest 45%.*

- From 1950 to 2010, the cost increased by *an astronomical 648%!*

- Which means that from 1900 to 2014, tuition + room and board for UPenn increased by *an unbelievable 986%!*

In addition to the NCES (2009) report, the ACTA (2009) findings confirmed a disturbing correlation first exposed in the ISI (2006) report: *the higher the tuition, the lower the general education requirements.*[228]

- The average tuition + fees at the 11 schools requiring NO general education subjects was $37,700.

- The average tuition + fees at the 5 schools requiring SIX general education subjects was $5,400.

- Overall, the average tuition + fees at the top national universities and liberal arts colleges was $35,000 per year...*yet they earned an average grade of "F."*

Also...bear in mind that *it now takes an average of six years* to graduate from college.

---

[228] http://www.goacta.org/publications/.../WhatWillTheyLearnFinal.pdf.

According to the National Inflation Association (NIA), during the 2009-2010 school year:[229]

- "Top 100 Colleges by Highest Tuition" (2008-2009) cost an average of *$42,173 (2014 USD)* per year.

- Private "4-year" colleges (2008-2009) cost an average of *$33,861 (2014 USD)* per year.

- Public "4-year" colleges (2008-2009) cost an average of *$15,441.60 (2014 USD)* per year.

Additionally, both *student loan debt and taxpayer funding* of "higher education" has risen considerably:

- Every year, collegians take out *$106 billion in student loans* and according to the Federal Reserve Bank of New York (as of August 2013) the *total U.S. student loan debt was $1.2 trillion.*[230]

- Total taxpayer funding of higher education, rose from *$117 billion (2014 USD)* in **1985** to *$286 billion in 2014…an increase of 144%!*[231]

- According to The Institute for College Access and Success (TICAS) "Project on Student Debt", *the average borrower will graduate with $26,600 in student loan debt.*

BOTTOM LINE: American colleges and universities are *shamefully* UNDER-producing and *unconscionably* OVER-charging.

---

229 http://inflation.us/collegebubble.html. Accessed 16 November 2011.
230 http://www.forbes.com/sites/specialfeatures/2013/08/07/how-the-college-debt-is-crippling-students-parents-and-the-economy/.
231 http://www.cato.org/pubs/pas/pa686.pdf. Accessed 21 November 2011. Cf. https://www.insidehighered.com/news/2015/06/12/study-us-higher-education-receives-more-federal-state-governments.

QUESTION 36

So what exactly does a college degree do for you?

Depends upon who you ask…but apparently, not much.

Richard Vedder, Distinguished Professor Emeritus of Economics at Ohio University, Director of the Center for College Affordability and Productivity, Adjunct Scholar at the American Enterprise Institute (AEI), and former economist with Congress' Joint Economic Committee, cited some *sobering numbers* from the Bureau of Labor Statistics (BLS):[232][233]

According to the BLS, in 2012, the U.S. labor force had…

- ❑ 481,206 customer service representatives
- ❑ 341,410 secretaries and administrative assistants (except legal, medical, and executive)
- ❑ 323,223 waiters and waitresses
- ❑ 207,665 executive secretaries and executive administrative assistants
- ❑ 136,305 receptionists and information clerks
- ❑ 115,520 janitors and cleaners (except maids and housekeeping cleaners)
- ❑ 107,546 laborers and freight, stock, and materials movers
- ❑ 83,028 bartenders
- ❑ 80,240 heavy and tractor-trailer truck drivers

---

[232] http://www.bloomberg.com/news/2012-06-17/end-u-s-student-loans-don-t-make-them-cheaper.html. Accessed 25 August 2012.
[233] http://centerforcollegeaffordability.org/research/studies/12-inconvenient-truths. Accessed 25 August 2012.

- ❑ 78,302 landscaping and grounds-keeping workers
- ❑ 73,124 carpenters
- ❑ 61,406 amusement and recreation attendants
- ❑ 56,959 food preparation workers
- ❑ 55,933 construction laborers
- ❑ 52,326 telemarketers
- ❑ 42,755 postal service mail carriers
- ❑ 40,967 electricians
- ❑ 38,903 hotel, motel, and resort desk clerks
- ❑ 26,879 flight attendants
- ❑ 16,138 parking lot attendants

...*with at least a bachelor's degree.*

There is absolutely nothing wrong with honest work, but there IS *something wrong with educrats squandering a student's potential.*

As Abraham Maslow once said, "If you plan on being anything less than you are capable of being, you will probably be unhappy all the days of your life."

Can anyone seriously suggest that those *2,420,015 people* attended college for *an average of six years* while incurring *an average student loan debt of $26,600* to find professional fulfillment...in the jobs listed above?

The BLS also reported that:

- ❑ In 2012, 53% of recent college graduates were either *unemployed or under-employed.*[234]

Educrats are deeply enamored with the oft-quoted and misleading statistic that, "over their lifetimes, college graduates earn more than non-graduates."

---

234 Jordan Weissmann, "53% of Recent College Grads Are Jobless or Underemployed—How?", *The Atlantic* (23 April 2012).

However, even high school students who are *fully qualified* to attend college are *increasingly unlikely* to derive enough professional benefits to justify the often six-figure cost and the six years it typically takes to graduate.

Furthermore, how much longer can ivory tower elites continue claiming (with a straight face) that bright, motivated "college-bound" students with advantageous family connections *owe the income difference to college*?

It is precisely those characteristics that enable them to attend college in the first place that improve their employment prospects, *not the degree they earn*.

QUESTION 37

How does "education" ultimately impact our nation's civic values?

In 2010, ISI published "The Shaping of the American Mind: The Diverging Influences of the College Degree & Civic Learning on American Beliefs."

"Same-sex couples should be allowed to legally marry."

- ❏ 24.6% of high school graduates agreed
- ❏ 39.1% of college graduates agreed
- ❏ 45.6% of those earning master's degrees agreed
- ❏ 42.8% of Ph.D.'s agreed

"Public school teachers should be allowed to lead prayers in school."

- ❏ 56.6% of high school graduates agreed
- ❏ 39.4% of college graduates agreed
- ❏ 30.3% of those with master's degrees agreed
- ❏ 17.0% of Ph.D.'s agreed

"Abortion should be available at any stage and for any reason."

- ❏ 21.0% of high school graduates agreed
- ❏ 20.8% of college graduates agreed
- ❏ 24.9% of those with master's degrees agreed
- ❏ 32.6% of Ph.D.'s agreed

"With hard work and perseverance anyone can succeed in America."

- ❏ 75.2% of high school graduates agreed
- ❏ 67.8% of college graduates agreed
- ❏ 64.2% of those with master's degrees agreed
- ❏ 50.8% of Ph.D.'s agreed

"The Bible is the Word of God."

- ❏ 74.2% of high school graduates agreed
- ❏ 63.5% of college graduates agreed
- ❏ 52.0% of those with master's degrees agreed
- ❏ 45.9% of Ph.D.'s agreed

Depending on your personal worldview…these results are either affirming or alarming.

QUESTION 38

What should the purpose of education be?

There is no perfect answer to that question since it depends upon a person's unique God-given passions and talents. However, it is also quite clear that compulsory government schooling was not designed to nurture the human potential of an individual.

George Washington, who believed that a national university would honorably serve several civic purposes, offered one possible answer:

❏ It would have helped students from all regions of the country "in acquiring knowledge in the principles of Politics and good Government."

❏ It would have alleviated the need for the nation's best and brightest to finish their education overseas, where they might be tempted to adopt "not only habits of dissipation and extravagance, but principles unfriendly to Republican Government and to the true and genuine liberties of mankind."

❏ It would have developed national unity by producing graduates who could "free themselves in a proper degree from those local prejudices and habitual jealousies which... when carried to excess, are never failing sources of disquietude to the Public Mind, and pregnant of mischievous consequences to this Country."

The brilliant Sir Ken Robinson offered this sage prescription:

"The fact is that given the challenges we face; education doesn't need to be reformed—**it needs to be transformed**. The key to this transformation is **not to standardize** education, but **to personalize it**, to build achievement on **discovering the individual talents of each child**, to put students in an environment where they **want to learn** and where they can **naturally discover their true passions**."[235]

The point here is *not* to tell parents how to educate their children. Educrats already do that *ad nauseum*. Instead, the point is to *liberate* parents from the dark agenda of compulsory government schooling and empower them to become *confidently intentional* in directing *their children's* educational future.

There is certainly no shortage of better alternatives.

[Full disclosure] My wife and I have homeschooled our daughter since she was four years old. But regardless of what you choose for your child's education, remember that no one loves them more than YOU do…and no one is more committed to their success than YOU are.

If you do decide to explore the idea of homeschooling your children, there are any number of excellent curriculums to choose from. However, I consider Leigh Bortins' *Classical Conversations*, **Andrew Pudewa's** the *Institute for Excellence in Writing (IEW)*, and **Andrew Kern's** *Lost Tools of Writing* to be among the best.

My advice to parents is simply this:

❑ Research *all* your options (there are several great alternatives to choose from).

---

235 Sir Ken Robinson, *The Element: How Finding Your Passion Changes Everything* (New York, NY: Penguin Group, 2009).

❏ Be willing to experiment (a lot) in order to find the option that (1) best fits your child and (2) best complements the values of your family.

❏ As you experiment with the options you choose, *be patient and kind to yourself*…because even the most well-intentioned experiments won't always work out the way you'd like. Just keep trying until it does.

Final thoughts…

To restore the Founding Fathers' vision of developing virtuous, free-thinking individuals who value liberty…we must TRANSFORM the way our children are educated. And though the effort to do so will not end with us, it must start somewhere.

> If your plan is for one year, plant rice.
> If your plan is for ten years, plant trees.
> If your plan is for one hundred years, educate children.
> CONFUCIUS (551-479 BC)

My wife and I founded Preparing Kids For Life (PK4L) because we believe that parents are unsung heroes who have the most important and most rewarding job in the world. (Of course, you would never know that by the way society maligns the family at every opportunity).

In fact, as parents…everywhere you turn, the world is saying that you don't have what it takes to raise your kids. That you're going to mess them up. That you're not "qualified" enough. At PK4L, we beg to differ.

Our mission is to remind parents that they *already have exactly what it takes* to prepare their kids for life as the best version of themselves. We want parents to reclaim their rightful place as the number one expert on their own children. All they need is the mindset. Let us show you how.

Parenting is truly the toughest job you'll ever love...but it's also a journey. And without a map, it's easy to get lost.

So, just think of us as your personal outfitters, guides, and allies for the road ahead. Your journey awaits. ☺

Please visit **www.welcomePK4L.com** to download your FREE eBook, *Building An Emotionally Healthy Home* as our gift to you.

P.S. For John Taylor Gatto..."Long live Bartleby!"

ACKNOWLEDGMENTS

In the brief space provided here, it is impossible to thank all those whose influence inspired the writing of this book that was ten years in the making.

However, this project would have never begun without the inspiration of Dani Johnson. God used her to restore a dream that I had thought long-lost and forgotten...I am forever in her debt.

To John Taylor Gatto, whose wisdom and insight opened my eyes to the tragedy of compulsory government schooling and saved me from passing that tragedy on to my students...I profoundly regret that I never had the honor of meeting him.

To Leigh Bortins, whose confidence in my book idea unlocked unimagined opportunities. I believe her vision for classical education will prove an important antidote to government schooling that our ailing nation so desperately needs.

To John Loeffler, for an incredible hour-and-a-half phone conversation that re-confirmed I was on the right path.

To James Lloyd, for his timely advice and generous encouragement.

To my incomparable wife Vicki, whose absolute belief in me is more than I deserve.

To my beautiful daughter Landry, who belongs to the generation this book is attempting to save.

To Erik Thureson and Joseph Dindinger, words are cheap substitutes to describe my gratitude for their loyal friendship. This project would not have happened without their steadfast support.

To my students, whose uncertain futures and untapped potential motivated me to persevere.

And lastly, to you the reader, the *number one expert on your own children*...and the molder and shaper of their dreams.

As C. S. Lewis noted, "You can't go back and change the beginning, but you can start where you are and change the ending."

Wherever you are in the journey of parenting, I hope this book empowers your path forward.

ABOUT THE AUTHOR

The author lives in Austin, Texas and is blessed to be the husband of Vicki, the father of Landry, and a die-hard fan of Real Madrid CF. For more information about his speaking events, resources, and general musings…

🌐 **Website** @ www.PK4L.com

🎙 **Podcast** @ https://anchor.fm/daniel-hagadorn

✉ **Contact** @ dh@PK4L.com

www.ingramcontent.com/pod-product-compliance
Lightning Source LLC
Chambersburg PA
CBHW070849050426
42453CB00012B/2113